ENDORSEMENTS

"Jack stands [out] in my mind as one of the captains [who]...thought outside of the box to...[harvest]...fish in the most efficient way and deliver the highest quality product. He was a pleasure to work with and always presented a positive attitude in a high-stress environment."

— Dave Abbasian, Western Alaska Operations, Trident Seafoods Corporation

"I have...watched [Jack] turn young greenhorns into seasoned deckhands, and [those] deckhands into old salts. Combine that with a lifetime on the water and surfing in... many countries, [Jack is] truly a waterman's waterman. The Bering Sea is not the same without Jack in it."

— Captain Jim Howard

"For years I had the pleasure of working alongside Capt. Jack Molan and his lovely wife, Joanne. We looked forward to having Capt. Jack come alongside to offload his catch because his fish were the best we ever processed. Also, he always saved three to four...king salmon for me to smoke! I'm retired now, and I miss those summer days visiting with... Joanne and Capt. Jack. We have a lot of sea stories to tell."

— Captain Joe Pirak

"[In my thirty-three years working in the Bering Sea], [a]long the way there have been certain captains that [have] had great, positive, and lasting influence on my career as well as the decisions I make every day to keep my crew safe and boat afloat in some of the most treacherous waters in the world. One of the most influential...is Captain Jack Molan. [H] is guidance was both appreciated and respected as his many years at the helm, with an exemplary safety record, were extremely valuable to myself or anyone on my deck...Thank you, Captain Jack, for all your thoughtful instructions and advice. My boat and crew are safer because of you!

— Captain Simon E. Burn, from the wheelhouse of *Ocean Hope 3*

Fishing Vessel (F/V) Columbia 123-foot Marco. Built 1980 Seattle,
Washington. King Crab 1980-1985, Trawler 1985 to present.
Jack was hired as a greenhorn in late 1979, engineered 1981-1987,
and was Capt Jack on the Columbia from 1987-2013.

Photo by: Craig Jenssen, Capt F/V Dominator

You can't make this stuff up

SARA
THANKS SO MUCH!
CAPT JACK :)

My Thirty Years
as Captain in the
Bering Sea

Capt Jack Molan

Printed in the United States of America

First Printing, September 2017

ISBN 978-0-9980196-0-4

A big thanks to David Marty for his talent and mad skills
in creating the awesome cover and layout for this book.
www.soundviewdesign.com

To my wife, Joanne,
my cheerleader and loving support
of thirty-six years,

and my dad, Keith Molan,
from whom I learned leadership,
respect, and honesty. I carried those
things with me on every voyage
in the Bering Sea.

ACKNOWLEDGMENTS

I'd like to acknowledge many of the people who've made this book possible. By attempting to mention everyone by name, I'll surely leave out many of you. If you were there, you know it. You're not forgotten. Thank you.

First and foremost, my wife, Joanne, after thirty-six years of marriage still encourages me to go for it. Her energy and love motivate me to push into new ventures. She's the reason I have stories to tell. Without her, I'd still be kicking rocks off the dock, dreaming. I love you, Joanne.

Our son, Gustav, his wife Ashley, our daughter, Ahna, her husband, Zach, and our younger daughter, Kirdy have never wavered in their encouragement from the time I floated the idea of writing. Your support and love mean the world to me. I couldn't have done this without you.

My editor and writing coach, Trish Wilkinson, carved out time to fit me in and exercised her amazing gift, interpreting what I tried to say. I've tested her limits with my bumbling prose. She has been thoroughly professional with both Joanne and me in pouring out her heart to make this the best possible book. You're a trooper, Trish. Thank you so much.

Writing is not a solo event. There's so much back and forth, working through ideas. Along my path, I've received unselfish help from Laura Meryl Herring and Kathy Stohrer. Both have given their time and creative energies to many of my stories yet to come. Thanks so much, my friends. Writing is something I've always thought I might do. It's a trip to learn the craft.

Finally, I'd like the thank our Creator. Life is precious. I've had a few wake-up calls in my years working out on the edge. It's said there are no atheists in life rafts. True or not, when faced with mortality, life gets a whole lot more valuable. Hang onto to those you love.

— *Captain Jack Molan, Bend Oregon, Sept. 2017*

AUTHOR'S NOTE

Dear Reader,

I have re-created events, locales, and conversations from my memories of them. Occasionally, I have changed the names and identifying characteristics of some individuals, including physical details, occupations, and places of residence to maintain anonymity.

— Capt. Jack

TABLE OF CONTENTS

Resolve – Captain Born...1

Patience – A Wicked Winter Night........................9

Emotional Control – Black Ship 15

Think Independently – Captain Chaos 23

Decisiveness – Time To Go....................................33

Courage – Taking Charge.......................................41

Faith – Alaska Grows Gus.......................................55

Teamwork – A Brush With Primal Fear 63

Gratefulness – A Life At Sea 69

Empowering Beliefs – Afraid of What? 79

RESOLVE

*Sometimes captains make calls that can put a crew in danger. In life,
how well we keep our cool in difficult situations, and* respectfully *share
what we know, can make the difference between success and failure. As a
young engineer on the Columbia, I was forced to confront authority on a
long stormy night when our lives hung in the balance.*

Captain Born

Weary from flying to this remote outpost in the Aleutian Islands, I jam my hands in my jeans' pockets. My coat inflates in the gusts and I shiver. Appearing through sea spray, the Columbia, pride of the fleet, turns into the bay. This fishing boat is my second home. I've spent three good years on board.

A few days ago, a call to Mom's house in Salt Lake City cut my Utah ski vacation short.

"Hey, Jack, we need an engineer. Can you make it?"

I thought, why not? It's got a new skipper and crew, but it's still an awesome boat.

As the king crab vessel approaches the dock, the crew, dressed in bulky orange exposure suits to ward off the extreme cold, throw lines the circumference of my forearm. Scrambling in tennis shoes, trying not to slip, I grab the frozen lines barehanded. My palms sting and my fingers go stiff, but I'd never complain.

I shout a quick hello to five deckhands as I toss my rubber duffel bag over the rail and spot Chip. He was the new kid three years ago. Now at twenty-one, he's become a top deckhand.

"Hey, Chipper," I say, shaking his gloved hand. "Good to see you. How's it going?"

He glances sideways. "Okay, Jackson. We're making money, dude."

Leaving my bag on deck below the wheelhouse, I bound up the ice-crusted steps to meet my new captain. Snow swirls around me as I enter, and a sour, locker room smell hits me so hard, I hold my breath. Empty plates and crumpled papers clutter the counters. I can barely see through the grime on the windows. This isn't the same vessel, my home, always a high-liner, a top boat.

In the command chair, the captain talks on the radio in boxer shorts and a t-shirt. His massive gut rubs against the console, and his butt cheeks sag off the edge of the chair. He glances my way, making no effort to wave or nod, and it dawns on me that he's the source of the stench.

The captain carelessly drops the microphone on the counter and says, "You must be Jack. We're taking off in a minute. Better get in the engine room. The last engineer was a piece of crap." He turns away without even shaking my hand.

I leave the wheelhouse, grateful to breathe without fighting my gag reflex, and grab my bag on deck. I walk aft toward the stern and carefully descend ice-covered steps—steps that should be cleared. At the bottom, huddled under an overhang, all five of the crew are smoking.

We shake hands and exchange names. A pimple-faced kid informs me he's Sean, the captain's nephew. With a cigarette in his lips, he nods proudly over my shoulder. "Check it out: 220 crab pots. I stacked 'em all myself."

Wary of pots piled unevenly, I barely muster a half-smile. King crab pots are seven-by-seven feet. Empty, they weigh more than 800 lbs. To stack them safely takes years of experience.

I duck into the empty galley where an overhead light is burnt out, and dirty dishes cover the counters. Down the hall, I flip on the light to the engineer's quarters and groan at the greasy coveralls strewn on the floor and candy wrappers scattered on sweat-stained sheets. Heaving a sigh, I drop my bag and turn off the light. My room will have to wait.

What have I gotten myself into with this new captain? I better get to the engine room.

At the engine room door, Chip stops me. "We're taking off right away," he says with apologetic eyes.

I can tell he wants to say more, but the boat starts moving. I don ear cups to deaden the clamor of machinery and slide down the ladder. Even in the dim light, I see the soot from a cracked exhaust pipe clinging to oil leaking from the engines. Black goo coats the floor and equipment. I want to cry.

The Columbia had been the Cadillac of vessels. The walls and engines were bright white. The aluminum floors sparkled. Now, slipping on grimy walkways, the engine room feels like a dungeon. I want to grab my bag and run. A dirty boat is an unsafe boat. Inhaling deep to bolster my courage, I grope in dark cabinets to find flashlights. All three have dead batteries.

Reluctantly, I put on a greasy headlamp. Surrounding me are four diesel engines, huge pump systems, electrical generators, fuel systems, fresh water pumps, refrigeration compressors, hydraulics, and tool boxes. Everything I touch is coated in a dark, slimy film. Scrubbing with degreaser will take weeks to get the engine room back to the way I left it.

Ignoring my revulsion, I check the fuel–how much and is it clean? I inspect oil levels, the engine temperature, compressors, and pumps. I secure all the valves controlling the critical ballast, assess the freshwater supply, and make sure the backup generator is working. After tuning up the equipment, I climb the stairs, wiping the handrail with a rag as I go.

The crew are in their bunks, yet the galley still reeks of old food. I take the long stairway up to the wheelhouse to see if I can get a read on my new captain. Instead, Sean sits at the controls on watch.

"Where are we headed?" I ask.

He pulls out his earbuds and shrugs. "I dunno. My uncle told me to go this way."

Gritting my teeth, I turn my head. This captain has no idea how to run a boat. I go below before I say something I'll regret.

In my smelly room, I pull off the soiled sheets and toss out a sleeping bag on the mattress. I'm exhausted after two days of flying and rescuing the engine room. Sleep comes instantly.

A beeping phone startles me awake. "Something's wrong," says the captain's whiney voice. "Check the engine room."

The boat goes weightless off the top of a wave, like an elevator dropping. As I'm getting off my bunk, my body gets tossed on the floor, and I crash against the opposite wall. Gaining my feet, I grab onto the railing, fumble along the hall, and go down the ladder—but no machinery appears out of place.

My stomach revolts with the boat's constant tossing on the rough sea, and I run up to the deck to puke. Wiping my chin, I see a wall of crab pots stacked thirty feet above my head, rocking and swaying. Terror grips me.

Crab pots shouldn't budge when they're tied together right. This stack should ride as if it's part of the boat, but the pots slam against each other with every roll. I lose what's left in my stomach and rush to the wheelhouse.

"Hey, what's wrong in the engine room?" the captain barks, dressed in boxers.

"Engine room is fine—the stack is loose," I choke out, gagging on his sweaty stench.

He rotates his chair and looks out the smeared window. "They'll be okay. We have twelve hours to get where the fishing is good. Just take care of the engine room. That's your department." Turning to his radio, he lets me know the discussion is over.

My mouth goes dry. A captain's word is law. Those crab pots could tip the boat. We could roll over and die. Sweat beads on my forehead. Staring at the loose pots, I lurch a dry heave.

"Hey, if you—" the captain starts.

Shots like gunfire interrupt as the chains holding the pots burst apart. Freed of constraints, the top half of the stack sways out over the edge of the boat. The shifting weight heels us sickeningly sideways. I bolt downstairs to the crew's quarters and slam open their doors. "Move it, guys," I yell. "We got problems."

"Chain down the stack," the captain's voice pounds over the loudspeaker. "Do it right this time."

"The stack is jumping too much," I tell the five groggy men. "It's impossible to get chains on. We have to get the pots off. Let's go tell the captain—"

"No way, Jackson. We don't tell that captain nothing," says a dazed Chip.

"He better listen, or this may be our last trip." I leave to stomp back up the stairs.

"What are you doing?" the captain shouts. "Get those chains on."

"We have to kick the pots overboard, and then haul and re-stack them."

"Who the hell do you think you are?" he says, fat neck bulging, his face beet red. "Chain up. You're wasting time."

I swallow bile and try to explain without yelling, "The stack is coming apart. If more chains break, it'll roll us over."

He points a thick, flabby arm at the door. "Get on deck!" he bellows.

As the crew scrambles to get into their deck suits, the loudspeaker booms, "Okay, pussies. We'll dump these pots and re-stack them. Make it fast."

Chip is the first to stagger outside. "I don't know how you did it, Jackson, but let's toss some pots," he says with a smile.

Seawater heaves across the deck, and ice-covered pots glow in the floodlights. The crew and I struggle to remain upright, clinging to railings and pipes, any handholds as the three-story monster flops and leans above us. The crew swing hammers to clear the ice on deck while Chip and I study the stack to plan our horrid task ahead.

Once we come up with a strategy to fix this mess, I say, "Chip, you're the best. No mistakes, kid."

"Hope my hands hold up, Jackson." His thin gloves offer little protection but are more flexible for gripping the ice-caked pots. Grabbing a baseball bat from the gear locker, he grins and slips a knife between his teeth. He winks as he wiggles his fingers, like a kid saying goodbye.

Chip steps out on the deck and begins climbing the wall of netting and rusty steel bars. Swinging the bat with one hand, he pounds the ice-covered web, clearing spots to hang onto. He kicks footholds into the ice and strains for his boots to find traction. Battling for each handhold, he inches higher where the motion wickedly intensifies—slamming, bucking, jumping.

He slips and hangs by one arm. The bat drops. Lightning quick, he traps it with his leg. His swinging arm flops at his side with fatigue, but he grabs the bat again and continues to bash at the ice and to climb.

I slip across the frozen upper deck and reach the controls to the crane. In this storm, getting the hook on the cable to hit my target will be like shooting basketballs at a moving hoop.

On top of the stack, Chip works a pot free from the ice with his bat. I swivel the head of the crane within a foot of his hand. He snatches the swinging hook and clips it to the pot. Grabbing the knife from his teeth, he cuts the ties. Like a whip, the stack jumps. Freed of constraints, the pot leaps, aimed at Chip. He dives, face down on top of the heaving stack, clinging for life.

A hellish block of steel and ice rushes at his prostrate body. He clutches the steel bars and webbing, bracing for impact. I yank hard on the crane controls, and the pot swoops over Chip, clearing him by inches.

I land the pot on the launcher, a wide table of steel pipe. The crew unhooks the crane, and deploys the first pot into the water. We all cheer as the crew tosses buoys and line to mark the location. We can do this!

Standing rock steady, straining at the crane controls for fifteen hours, every muscle aches with cold and exhaustion. The last pot goes overboard and everyone whoops, fists in the air, triumphant.

Without food, drink, or bathroom breaks, the six of us vanquished the beast.

My toes may be numb, but relief floods my soul. We've survived.

The deck speaker blasts: "You girls took forever. Stack 'em right from now on."

That voice. That disrespect. It's my life-changing moment.

I'm going to become a Captain.

I'll respect my boat and my crew.

And I'll do everything I can to keep them safe.

PATIENCE

Call on patience when surrounded by fury. Calm the confusion of the moment. Pull back. Take a breath. Decide whether you need more information to make a good decision, and actively seek to understand. But like most things, patience requires balance. Be aware that fear can masquerade as patience. Do I stand by, or should I go? Your crew, business associates, or classmates will wait on you if you're the leader. Be careful not to get stuck at the dock, afraid to move.

A Wicked Winter Night

The Columbia pounds through challenging waves. The gale blows sea spray across our decks that flash freezes, adding weight to the boat. Having delivered our last load of fish, we're enduring the 200-mile return to our fishing area.

Boats can roll in icing conditions, but if I continue at reduced speed in the inky black night, the spray should be manageable. Squinting at the chart, my eyes burn from being awake for twenty-four hours. I plot a course skirting the peninsula separating the North Pacific and Bering Sea, keeping the trawler five miles from land.

The first watch arrives in the wheelhouse to relieve me: Johnny, our youngest crewman at twenty-four. His dark eyes look brighter after a few hours' sleep.

"If the wind picks up or the temp drops, wake me," I say and go below deck to catch a nap.

I fall asleep instantly and am startled awake when I hear, "Capt, you better take a look."

Fully dressed, I roll up and over the high-sided bunk to rush after Bobby, the deck boss, up the short staircase, into the wheelhouse. The hair rises on the back of my neck. We have no visibility on the starboard side. High on the mast, our crab lights accentuate the ice crystals that obscure the windows. Stepping to the port side, I see less ice and purse my lips, forcing air out slowly.

We're in trouble.

Sea spray and plunging temperatures have added tons of ice to the starboard side, while fierce winds brace the heavy side, hiding the imbalance. Young Johnny hadn't noticed, but Bobby spotted the problem as soon as he came on watch.

Without looking at Bobby I say, "Get the guys up. We got work to do."

We're in for an ice busting party.

"Roger that, Capt." Bobby dives downstairs to shake the crew awake.

The boat is upright, but stability is tenuous. The thick ice makes us top heavy.

If the wind against our heavy side changes, we're sunk.

"Everything's okay as long as everything's okay," I recite several times. Sayings like this have kept me alive, and my next moves have to be right. The closer I can get us to shore, the milder the waves will be, reducing the spray, which will diminish the ice buildup.

The autopilot holds us on course. I dare take five steps from the console to brew a strong cup of java, breathing deep to remain calm. Setting the cup in its holder, I jump in the wheelhouse chair, pulling back the throttles to slow the boat. Wind noise thrums through the antennas above my head. Spires play different tones as gusts rise and fall.

I hope to spot another vessel within fifty miles using the automatic identification system (AIS). But the screen is blank. On the vast frigid ocean, our vessel is a lonely speck of light, a thin skin of steel on the tumultuous sea holding warmth and life.

Sipping my coffee, I peer through ice-crusted windows, beyond the sodium floodlights, and see nothing but black water streaked with white spray. We wouldn't survive five minutes out there.

Grabbing the ship phone, I press the button. "Guys, come up when you're done getting coffee."

I put my hand on the knob, ready to change course and force myself to wait, to think it through. My mind screams: *get closer to land*. But I'm torn.

"Turning toward land may roll us over," I mumble.

The bow pitches up. Spray covers us in more deadly ice. Then we drop, slamming against the water. I squeeze the arms on my chair to keep my seat and hear a crewman curse in the galley. My heart races, and my hand tenses on the knob.

"Easy, Jack," I scold myself aloud, releasing my grip on the control. "Fear kills. Cool heads prevail."

I have to finesse the boat toward shore. It's our best shot at survival.

My weary crew climbs the stairs with one hand on the rail and one clutching a coffee cup. "Hey guys, how ya doing?"

"Another day in paradise, huh, Captain?" The ship's engineer, Greg, smiles over the steam curling from his cup.

"Roger, Greg," I say. "Everything good down below?"

"Roger, Capt. All good." Greg takes a swig of coffee.

"Okay, boys, we're heavy with ice on the starboard side. The wind's been holding us up, so we've got to head toward land, and you'll have to break out the anchor."

The guys nod slowly.

Downing the last of my cold coffee, I drop the cup in the holder. Dire situations like this bring on my laser focus, an otherworldly perception that guides me. I'm ready to make a move. "Let's see how she likes a course change."

I click in a ten-degree adjustment.

The bow swings smartly to the right. The droning antennas change tune. Wind no longer blows directly on our side, and spray pelts the front windows. The boat dips slightly starboard. My stomach muscles tighten.

"Needs to be more direct." Checking the Radar and Plotter, I sigh. "Okay, let's see if she'll go another ten degrees."

I dial the course change slowly, a few degrees at a time. Our lights reveal wind and spray on the forward quarter as the vessel lists alarmingly to the right. My boat tells me: that's enough. After years in the chair, I know her limits.

"Like a ball balanced on the nose of a seal," I joke and light a cigarillo, contemplating my options. Snapping the lighter shut—

wham. A gust slams our port side. I'm thrown against the window, staring at the ocean a foot below the glass. It's a surreal view as the boat rises and falls in the swells, laying on its side.

Ship alarms go off. Pinned between a window and the boat's controls, I can't reach the handles. Our forward motion pushes us under water. I grunt, forcing my torso to twist enough to pull the throttle to idle. The wind changes direction and stops the rolling, but we still lay on our side like a wounded animal.

Helpless to save the Columbia or my crew, a dreamlike sensation engulfs me, and I beg God to keep the wind on our right side. Inch by excruciating inch, the boat lifts, fighting the waves to pull herself upward. With a survivor's heart, she rights herself.

I feel the entire crew exhaling with me. Dropping in my chair, I grip the armrests, clinging to a familiar thing. "Everyone okay?" I call out.

Two guys are sprawled on the floor.

"Yeah, all good, Capt," says Greg. "That sucked. I spilled my coffee. Sorry. I'll shampoo the carpet later." Unable to see his expression in the dim light, I can imagine his grin.

"Greg, go down to check the bilges, and make sure we're watertight. And get started transferring fuel and water to the high side." I look at the two men getting to their feet. "Guys, look below to see if anything busted loose." I open the cabinet containing my survival suit. "A 123-foot Marco has never rolled over, but let's be on the safe side and get out our suits." I nod to my crew. "Okay, boys, we got this."

Damn. I should have taken these precautions earlier. We're lucky a good boat saved herself despite my mistakes.

Transferring fuel and water gives us stability. Setting a course for land, the smell of bacon pervades the wheelhouse, and my stomach growls. A big breakfast will keep the crew going today. There's a lot of work to be done before we can set our nets again.

The deadly conditions improve as we get closer to land. Although the boat is still relentlessly hammered by bitter wind, the spray has subsided, so the wicked ice accumulation has stopped. Surrounded by snow covered mountains, a crescent beach of black volcanic sand gives us protection. Sunrise paints the snowy peaks a pale pink.

Armed with ice mallets, we bundle up for a long day. Ice entombs the anchor requiring the crew to pound and hammer, freeing it of ice, to make the winch functional again. Heavy chain rattles over the bow roller as the anchor breaks through chunks of sea ice and bites into the sand at the bottom. We're secure. Our boat is safe.

In howling winds, we swing our massive hammers. Whump. Whack. Thump. The ice reluctantly releases its grip on the rails and decks. Weary crewmen shovel heavy loads into the sea throughout the day, muscles trembling with fatigue.

Cod fish soup and bread, prepared by Johnny the Portuguese, is devoured by a dog-tired crew. Smiling wind-burned faces surround me in the galley. We're all grateful to be alive.

"Good job today, boys." The crew watches me get up from the table, waiting for directions. "I'll take anchor watch. Everyone get some sleep. This blow will moderate by morning, so we'll fish tomorrow."

EMOTIONAL CONTROL

Fear can torpedo anyone's performance. Stress, anger, anxiety, and worry, all manifestations of fear, can cause us to make bad decisions or act irrationally. So, how do we get a handle on these emotions to get good results? As a captain in the Bering Sea, maintaining emotional control is critical. You may not find yourself in too many life-and-death situations, but you may find a technique to apply to your life in this story to empower you in times of anxiety.

Black Ship

A tiny alcove against a volcanic mountain protects our fishing boat from an angry Bering Sea. Still, the anchor chain snaps taut as sixty-knot winds batter the Columbia. Our powerful floodlights illuminate ice and snow, like millions of tiny comets playing tricks on my eyes. I plan to ride out this furious gale during the long Alaskan winter night—until the satellite phone rings, and a nervous voice comes through the speaker.

"Hey, Jack. Can you pick me up?" The numbers on the screen verify what I suspect. The voice is the captain's from the Alaska Gold, a 160-foot crab boat.

"Hey, Paul. How ya doing?"

"I got a problem. We got contaminated fuel, and we're black ship. I set the anchor, but I can't tell if it's holding. Can you give me a tow?"

Uh-oh. "Black ship" means he has no electricity or electronics to navigate in this maelstrom. I scan my radar screen and spot the Alaska Gold nine miles away. I grab the intercom. "We got a boat in trouble," I tell my crew. "Let's move out,"

I hear dishes drop in the sink and Bobby, the deck boss, yelling to Greg, our engineer, "Fire up! Someone's in trouble. Let's move it, guys."

My heart sinks when I get a positive fix on Paul's position, only twelve-hundred feet from a deadly rock reef. The wind will push the Alaska Gold onto the rocks if the anchor drags.

"Okay, Paul," I say into the satellite phone. "We're firing up and pulling anchor. We'll reach you in less than an hour. I have a lock on your position, and your anchor is holding."

"Thanks. Everything went black right after I woke up. I barely had time to spot you on radar. My backup batteries are dying, too."

The Columbia's powerful engine roars above the whistling wind. The second our anchor comes aboard, I crank a sharp turn and shove the throttle to full speed. Frigid waves pummel the bow, soaking the crew.

"Everyone to the wheelhouse as soon as possible," I call on the loudspeaker.

Coffee in hand, wearing coveralls, Greg arrives first from the engine room. The crew file up the stairs to the wheelhouse, breathing heavily from hauling the anchor. I hold out my hand, palm down, to signal them to be quiet and grab the mic. "We're headed at you, Paul. The navigation computer says forty-four minutes."

"Yeah, okay, Jack. I really need a tow."

Clad in rubber deck suits, the crew's wet faces glow in the dim blue light of the electronics. Johnny is a Portuguese man in his twenties with kind, dark eyes and scratchy five-day stubble. Thirty-year-old Bobby, having been on several rescues, instructs the crew about how to tow another vessel. Standing a head taller than his mates, Peter, a big blonde Swede, assures Bobby he knows where the attachments are stored to assemble a tow cable.

I put down the mic and turn to my crew. "Okay, boys, I appreciate the quick get-away—"

"It's so dark without radar," interrupts Paul's voice through the speaker. "I can't see where we are."

"I got you," I assure him. "You're holding tight, not moving at all."

"Yeah, okay, Jack."

Organizing my thoughts, I wipe the computer and radar screens with a flannel cloth.

"Here's the situation," I tell the crew. "The crabber Alaska Gold is black ship, hanging on anchor close to a nasty reef, with water in their fuel. The captain wants us to tow his boat, except hooking onto him, with his anchor down, could put us sideways in this heavy wind and toss us onto the rocks. A better option would be for them to siphon the water from the fuel tanks to get their engines running. Still, if the anchor slips, with a dead engine, they'll be pitched onto the reef and sink. We have to be ready to pull guys out of the water."

My crew stares at me with wary eyes.

"I'll tell you this, we will not be victims," I say. "Bobby, I want you and Peter to get the deck equipment ready in case we need to tow them. Johnny, you get all the MOB (man overboard) equipment out and ready—but don't do anything without hearing from me, okay? We have less than thirty minutes to get everything prepared, so let's go."

The guys head out on deck, talking strategy and delegating jobs.

I check on Alaska Gold's position, relieved her signature hasn't moved on my screen.

"Hey, Jack, how's it going?" says Paul's anxious voice through the speaker again.

"Won't be long now. Are you making headway cleaning up the fuel?"

"We've got eight fuel tanks, and the first three we tried have water. It takes time to check each one, so I sent out my crew with a torch to cut the anchor cable."

My mind screams: what's he *doing?* Cutting the cable could send his ship careening and get both our vessels smashed into the rocks. Aloud I say, "Uh...okay. What are you up to, Paul?"

"When you get a line on me, I'll cut our anchor cable, so you can tow us out of here."

He's scared. I understand, but his fear is making him irrational. "Have you got a life raft ready?" I ask. "Do your guys have their survival suits out?"

"Ah, no. We've been so busy."

"Paul, if this goes bad, you need to be ready to go in the water."

"Yeah, okay. I'll get one of my crew to do that."

"If it were me, instead of waiting for your signal to cut the cable,

I'd have the crew down helping your engineer. Your best bet is to clean up the fuel, or find a tank with clean diesel."

"Yeah, okay. Right. I better go see how they're doing."

Through the back windows, I glance at our two massive towing winches, each the size of a compact car, looming in the deck lights. Each has a mile of steel cable, an inch thick, leading from the winch to the stern, joined in a V-shaped bridal. Hopefully, I won't have to use them—and endanger my men.

"We'll see the Alaska Gold any second now," I call on the loud hailer.

The streaking snow obscures visibility, but out of the white flurry, the black ship appears in our bright lights. Eight- to ten-foot waves pitch our vessel as I approach their stern, coming a short distance alongside. An intense flash sparks on his bow—the cutting torch.

"Hey, Paul! What are you doing?" I shout into the microphone, but there's no answer. I shake my head, sucking air through clenched teeth.

"Jack, I see you," says Paul's voice an excruciating minute later. "Ready to hook up?"

Our boats bounce in dangerously steep swells, rising and falling out of sync. "Any luck on the fuel?" I ask.

"Nah. There's a lot of water. I don't know what happened..." His voice trails off.

Damn. I've got to keep him focused. "How about the survival suits? Did you get down a life raft?"

"Oh, no. Not yet. My guys are on the bow."

He's ready to cut his anchor with dead engines and no survival gear ready. The silhouette of the Alaska Gold pitches twenty-feet in the air and slams at the bottom of a swell. My boat's motion is as radical, but opposite. As my bow drops, his rises. Clouds of spray blow over both vessels.

To get attached to the Alaska Gold will be a monumental task. The messenger line will be swept away in the screaming winds, and we could be shoved sideways, out of control. If that happens, we'll both get pitched onto the reef.

"Hey, Jack, you there?"

"Roger, go ahead." I finger a small cigar, trying to settle my nerves.

"The torch won't stay lit in this wind. I sent them to look for a cutting wheel and grinder. I'm ready for a tow, Jack. Go ahead and come alongside."

"A grinder takes electricity, something you don't have," I remind him, lighting the cigar, trying to keep my cool.

"Oh, yeah," he says. "Jeez, what was I thinkin'?"

"You've got a lot on your mind. How 'bout that raft and those survival suits?"

"Uh...Let me look."

I roll my eyes as I admire my smoke ring—and see a wall of water rise outside the window. I snatch the loudhailer and yell, "Watch it guys! Wave coming!"

The bow hurls to the sky. My gut tightens as I squeeze the arm rests and spin my chair to see the deck. Three of the crew scramble forward to safety under an overhang. Peter, caught in the open on the stern, can't make the dash forward. He bolts to the ladder welded onto the back wall and bounds up like a cat. Four feet of icy seawater engulfs the deck. The massive cables on the winches slam to one side, and a five-gallon bucket flies overboard. Hanging onto the rungs, Peter wiggles his butt at the receding water that smacks against the wall just below him, and I laugh out loud, loosening the knot in my stomach.

"Hey, Jack, can you bring your lights to our stern?" says Paul's voice on the radio. "Our rafts are back there, and we can't see."

"Will do." Feeling bad for them, suffering in the dark on the cold, angry ocean, with the raucous wind and waves making communication near impossible, I put my boat in gear. The Columbia advances past their ship, and I pivot to illuminate the entire back of the Alaska Gold.

"The chief says he can try a generator in a few minutes," says Paul's hopeful voice. "He may have found some clean fuel."

"That's great news."

I see the crew fighting to get a life-raft free when—Pow! The Alaska Gold appears from the dark, the deck bathed in brilliant light.

"Hey, Jack, we got power!"

"Yeah, I see you. Very cool. That's got to feel good." Now they can see, use the bathroom, have heat, even warm up a burrito in the microwave.

"No kidding. The chief got the main engine running too."

"Great. Let the engine idle for a while to make sure it's purged of water. When you decide to pull out, I'll be right behind you for backup."

Pulling the anchor on the Alaska Gold goes slowly. The entire length of cable had been deployed when the emergency started, so we wait for ten anxious minutes. The crew and I monitor their progress from the wheelhouse.

"We're almost ready to try and pull out," says Paul's voice. My crew's heads turn toward the radio. Without the security of an anchor, Paul is dependent on one engine to beat back the angry sea and keep his ship off the rocks.

"This is the critical moment," I say. "Be ready to jump fast."

We hold a collective breath, watching the anchor come on board the other vessel. I bring the Columbia as close as I dare. We're ready to spring into action.

Gradually, the Alaska Gold pulls away from the reef and we follow. Each minute brings us further from danger and un-flexes a few more of my muscles. For the hour's passage to King Cove, we're poised to assist if anything else goes bad in this wicked winter storm. By the time we arrive in the protected bay, my eyes burn, and my butt aches in the captain's chair. "Thanks, Jack, and thanks to your crew," says the radio.

"Sure, Paul, glad it worked out. Goodnight."

We drop our anchor, and I tell my weary crew, "You guys were awesome. The fish are only a few hours from here, so we'll head out in the morning."

I put up my feet on the console and relight my cigar. Smoke curls and snakes in front of me as my tension drains.

Still, the wind shrieks past the windows. I envision the reef, both ships shoved onto the rocks, the dark surf relentlessly pounding us— and I feel grateful we'll see another dawn.

THINK INDEPENDENTLY.

A good leader won't get sucked into every situation. If you're in charge, you have to weigh the circumstances to make a solid decision. A seemingly harmless distraction on the surface can devolve into a life-and-death condition, figuratively or literally. That's the loneliness of command. The responsibility falls on you. It's your ship, your crew.

Captain Chaos

Solid spray batters the wheelhouse windows. My tired eyes strain to see in the dark night. The bow plunges, scooping sea-water in front of another huge wave. As the wave hits, the bow jumps, launching water over the wheelhouse. Free-falling into the trough of another twenty-foot swell, the sea-water, streaked with foam, rushes my vessel like storm troopers.

Illuminated under floodlights, my crew, in bright orange deck suits, works the back deck with agility and competence gained from years on the Bering Sea. A hundred tons of pollock spill from the net to add to the three fish holds, filling the Columbia to capacity—half-a-million pounds of fish chilled and ready for market.

"We extract protein from a hostile environment," I say aloud to myself with a grin.

I reach the volume knob on the radio without looking, listening again to the nasty forecast: winds at ninety knots, forty-five-foot swells. My stomach tightens. This angry sea will soon become diabolical.

Forty-eight hours earlier, safe in the harbor, I had struggled with my decision. Could I fill the boat and return before the bulk of the storm hit? I'd have to do everything right to miss the worst of it.

So far, my calculated gamble is working. I clutch the microphone, calling on deck: "Bobby, make sure everything is secure. The waves will get insane in a few hours."

From below my window, a bright orange arm shoots me a thumbs-up. The wheelhouse bucks and drops. I shuffle, bow-legged for stability, a few steps to the chart table. I grip the teak hand rails, the red chart light protecting my night vision as I plot a course for home. We'll run south, straight downwind, arriving in a protected harbor just ahead of the hurricane winds. We're in great shape to pull this off.

The radio crackles over the shrieking wind noise: "Hey, Jack. What's going on? You fill up? Is it blowing out there yet?"

I smile at my friend's voice. "You know it, Harry. We're full. Just cleaning up the deck. How ya doing, man?"

"I'm sitting at the dock. You did good, my friend."

"Roger that. Some days you're the big dog; some days you're the hydrant."

He laughs. "It's gonna blow like stink tonight. Be careful out there."

"Right on, Harry. Don't worry 'bout me. You know I'm a wuss." The intercom rings. "Hey, my crew is calling. I need to turn the boat and pay attention. See ya."

"The deck's ready, Capt," says my deck boss's winded but happy voice. "The holds are stuffed full."

"Okay, Bobby. Excellent. Thanks. Tell the guys, 'Good job,' and watch out down there. I have to get turned around, and I don't want anyone getting washed over."

I stand next to the wheelhouse chair, focusing on the towering swells. With one hand on the throttle and one on the steering, my knees dig into the console for stability. I exhale slowly, intensely studying the ocean, looking for a spot between swells where I can turn around.

As though time slows, I become part of the maelstrom. Timing is critical. If I get sideways in the huge waves, the water could sweep the boat and lay us over. I have to maneuver between swells as fast as possible—like driving across railroad tracks as soon as one train passes, then making a U-turn and crossing again before the next train. But I was designed to do this.

The boat climbs a colossal wave face. I strain to see the top. As we tip over the white-crested peak, I spot an opening. Now!

I jam the throttle to full power and turn the rudder hard as we drop down the backside of a liquid mountain, picking up speed. Another foam-streaked monster charges at us from out of the darkness. I pray, committed now, no holding back. C'mon baby. Move it. We're almost around. Move it!

The boat completes the turn just in time, and the thirty-foot swell rolls under our stern, pushing us forward. We're on course for home.

"Hey, Jack. You there?" shouts the speaker on the private satellite system rather than the two-way radio. "It's Lava Point. Captain Wally."

Lava Point is a small boat. He must be at the dock killing time till the storm passes. "Yeah, I got ya, Wally. Don't come out here. It's ugly and getting worse by the minute."

"No, no, Jack. I need you to stand by. I got problems."

I grab my gut as if someone sucker-punched me. Forcing myself to take a deep breath, I say, "What's up? Where are you?"

"I'm off the point in front of you. We're leaning over pretty bad."

"I'll be there in twenty minutes."

As I push the throttle to full speed I see him on radar, way too close to the rocks. What's he doing out here?

Johnny, my youngest deckhand, steps into the wheelhouse to check in. "Johnny, Wally's in trouble," I say. "Get the guys."

Rolling his eyes, Johnny dives down the stairs. Inside of a minute, all four crew have gathered near me. Bobby cut his shower short and towels his wet hair.

"The boards in the fish hold busted," says Wally's voice through the speaker. "The fish all slid to one side. The swells and fish are pushing us over."

Johnny shakes his head in what looks like disgust.

"What's up?" I ask.

"I worked for Captain Wally. He's crazy."

My crew mumbles in agreement.

"Big surprise," says Bobby. "Wally's is the only small boat out today, and now he's in trouble."

"Get the man overboard equipment ready: survival suits and both life-rafts," I tell them.

"Why two rafts, Captain?" asks Bobby. "Isn't one plenty for a boat like theirs?"

"The other raft is for us," I say, feeling tension from all four men.

"Capt Wally locks the crew out of the wheelhouse where they keep the survival suits," Johnny says. "If the boat rolls, they don't have a prayer."

My gut knots. "Thanks, Johnny. Let's hop to it, guys."

"Jeez, Capt." Bobby tosses up a hand. "We go from a perfect trip to needing a life raft in the blink of an eye."

"Yep. We've all trained for this. Let's go."

My voice sounds calm, but my mind sprints. A small boat near the rocks, in danger of rolling over in twenty- to thirty-foot swells, could endanger my crew as well. I have to weigh how much I'm willing to risk my own boat to save those guys.

I aim the floodlights forward and concentrate on guiding the Columbia through the heavy snow and growing waves. In the background, I hear sounds of the crew hustling suits out of the closet and rafts being removed from their racks on the deck outside. When they finish their assignments, the crew returns to the wheelhouse.

Pointing and gasping, we spot the Lava Point out the windows. The tiny vessel disappears between towering swells, heeling dangerously to the left with each wave, close to the rocks. I wince and blurt, "Oh crap. He's in some kinda trouble."

Another set of swells the size of a three-story building smash into the Lava Point, laying the boat further on its side. White water buries the back deck with each assault. The crew's fate looks grimmer with each successive swell that inches them closer to the ragged boulders.

"I see you, Jack," comes Wally's voice again from the speaker. "Looks like I got another problem."

Shaking my head, I glance at my quiet crew and grab the mic. "What's up, Wally?"

"My bilge is filling with water, and I can't leave the wheelhouse to pump it out."

"Have a crewman do it!" I shout out of reflex.

"Ah, no, Jack. No."

Johnny holds up his hands. "On that boat, no one except Wally is allowed in the engine room either."

"If no one can pump the bilge or drive the boat, Capt Wally is up a creek," I say.

"What is this?" Bobby crosses his arms. "This guy screws up left and right, and we have to risk our lives to save his butt?"

"Okay, boys, hold on." I look each one in the eye. "I'm not about to lose this boat or crew trying to do the impossible. None of you make a move without my say so."

The Lava Point slides up a wave face, coming up level as the wave passes. Wally calls in, "Jack, if I steer to the left, on top of the wave, it brings me upright."

My eyes go wide. "But doesn't that steer you closer to the rocks?"

"Roger that, Jack. But if I play with the steering and throttle, the boat stays more upright."

"His bilges are flooded, his load of fish shifted, and his boat heels further with every swell." I look over my radar at Johnny. "This guy is a real piece of work."

Johnny puffs air between his lips. "Yeah, he is."

"Wally, I'll call the Coast Guard," I say. "If you go on the rocks, I can't help you. Your only hope is a helicopter."

"Oh, no, Jack. Please don't call them. I'll be good as soon as I clear the point. I just have to get out of these big waves."

"It's why he called you on the satellite system," Johnny says. "It's private. He knows the Coast Guard would shut him down."

"Watch it, Capt," Bobby says and points over my shoulder.

I turn to see a thirty-foot, double-crested wall of water charging at us and grab the microphone to warn Wally. "A massive double-up is coming your way."

The back deck of my boat gets buried, but we have plenty of buoyancy to rise and shed the water. In horror, we watch the same wave engulf the Lava Point, rolling the vessel fully on its side. The second crest hits. The mast and antennas sink underwater, followed by the wheelhouse. A long moment passes as the little boat disappears under foam and black water. Deck boards, buoy bags, anything that isn't tied down spills into the sea. I can only imagine the terror the crew feels, hanging on in the galley.

My wheelhouse is silent as we stare at the propeller above the surface, turning slowly. I think: she's going down, stern first. Then slowly, the tiny vessel rises enough for the propeller to bite water. The Lava Point slowly moves forward, labors, severely heeling to the left once more.

A mere hundred yards separate the boat from the rocks. Progress to reach the point is excruciatingly slow. Wave after wave rolls over the tiny vessel, but somehow it recovers after each hit. The boat struggles onward with whitewater smashing against the cliffs in the background. Then two black towers of water converge from different directions, forming a pyramid under the vessel. The Lava Point lifts and begins sliding toward the rocks.

Game over. They're dead.

Except the boat doesn't surf, overloaded with bilge water and fish. The wedge-shaped nightmare passes, but another set of three waves, higher than any others, charge the point. I remain silent with my heart in my throat. I can do nothing to save them.

The Lava Point disappears behind the first giant. All eyes strain to see the small boat rise, but nothing. Two more monster waves pass, and still, there's no boat in sight. "That's too long without spotting them. Watch for anything floating, guys."

Then comes Wally's voice again. "Right on, Jack. Thanks for standing by. That last set of waves pushed me around the corner. I'm out of the big waves. Pretty cool, huh?"

My legs go weak. I slump in my chair, and a strange mix of anger and joy come over me.

"What the hell, boss?" Bobby blurts.

I put up a hand and answer Wally. "No problem. I'll accompany you to the dock, so you can get fixed up." As I drop the microphone, tension drains from me. I feel like a limp rag.

"Uh, no. I'm not going in, Jack. I'll anchor close by. We'll get her fixed up by morning. I want to go fishing tomorrow."

What? He needs to make real repairs. They have to get the fish off the boat.

My outrage must show because Johnny says, "Yep, that's how he is, Captain."

The other men nod again in agreement.

"Wally, that's cutting it too close, man," I say, now that we're in protected water. "How 'bout you follow me into the dock?"

"We got this now," Wally says. "Thanks for standing by. I really appreciate it."

I follow the Lava Point past the headland and watch him turn off to a small protected cove and anchor up. Once his boat seems as secure as it's going to be, I steer the Columbia on course to deliver our fish inside the harbor. With raw nerves, I brew a coffee, wondering: do I report Wally or call the boat's owner? The crew had no idea how close they came to sinking.

Like a sledgehammer, a ninety-knot gust hits the window next to my head, shocking me out of my stupor. My boat needs me. The storm has arrived in full force. I'm glad to be in the wheelhouse, away from the fury outside. I call Dave, the head guy at the fish processing plant.

"You better hold off until this wind passes," Dave says. "We're kicking all the boats off the dock now."

We drop anchor in a small cove, shielded from the waves. Hundred-knot winds screech through the rigging, sounding like an out-of-tune pipe organ, whipping the water into harmless spray. The droning noise relaxes me. Our boat is full, and we're safe from the hurricane—a job well done. Only a fisherman can relate to this particular feeling.

I can only imagine how hellish the storm is for the guys on the Lava Point with their imbalanced load. The laws can only regulate so much of fishing on the high sea. Dirty players participate, and life seldom goes well for them—or their crews.

DECISIVENESS

Harmony is the goal to keep an organization running smoothly.
A leader's job is to spot and deal with someone in the group who
undermines or ruins morale—that know-it-all, the one who often
complains, the one who second-guesses the others and bullies them.
Leaders have to be decisive and protect the group; that is,
figure out how to remove the person causing problems.

Time To Go

Approaching the pier, I maneuver the Columbia against the dock. My relaxed pace displays the morning mood. Small brightly colored homes of red, green, and yellow cling to hilly contours along the shore and reflect on the bay. My crew secures our vessel to steel piers backed by a concrete wall. Boardwalks span the deep grass and wildflowers, between the beach and the native Aleut village of five hundred, huddled at the edge of the Bering Sea.

Our tranquil arrival is interrupted by loud hellos and introductions between crew members and the new guy on the dock. Tom, our fleet manager, has sent Curt, a six-foot-three thirty-year-old wearing designer jeans. He clears the rail in one hop, hustles up the stairs to the wheelhouse and says, "Captain Jack, I'm Curt." His voice is as big as his smile. He drops a new sea bag at his feet and reaches out to shake hands. "Glad to meet ya."

I slide off the Captain's chair to greet him. "Welcome aboard, Curt. Good to have you. I'm glad you're on time because we'll have to depart before the tide gets too low."

Curt winks at me, sticks his head out the door, and whistles. "Hey, Johnny," he yells, "can you grab my bag?" Giving me a nod, he heads below to the galley. I hear, "Hey, there, I'm Curt. Are you the cook? I'm starving, man."

On the way out to sea, as I near the shallowest section of the channel, Curt appears, unannounced. His head hangs over my left shoulder, chewing a turkey sandwich. "Okay, Capt, ready to show me the controls?" he garbles with his mouth full.

"Not now. Stay back." I toss a scowl at him. "Don't block the radar."

Curt leans forward, in spite of my order, takes a huge bite, and mayo plops on my radar screen.

"Okay, Curt, clear out," I say through clenched teeth.

He grins with stuffed cheeks and walks past the chart table, dropping onto a pedestal chair on the far side of the wheelhouse. While I wipe at his mess with my bare hand, spreading goo across my screen and getting mayo between my fingers, he texts on his cell phone. Biting my lip, I try to ignore him and focus on navigating the shallow channel.

"Oh man." Curt swallows the last bite of his sandwich and burps. "Guess I'm about to fall into food coma. I'll see you later." With that, he disappears downstairs.

A few hours later, alone in the wheelhouse, I sip coffee and plan to call a few trusted captains on the radio to trade vital information: weather, fishing locations, and optimal gear. In quiet contemplation, I form my fishing strategy with the mindset of a predator—until Curt shows up.

"Hey, Capt, how ya doing?" he asks, tripping loudly on the top step, spilling his mocha on the wheelhouse carpet.

"Stay over there," I say, pointing to a chair on my far left.

"You need a driver tonight, I'm your man, Capt. The night guys on other boats all know me."

"We can talk about driving later." Or maybe never. Could this guy be any more annoying?

Our boat passes near a smaller vessel, and Curt hops off his chair. "Hey, the Topaz. My buddy Pauly is on deck." He bursts out the back door and hangs over the railing, sweatpants at his ankles, mooning the Topaz, howling with laughter. The Topaz crew returns the salute.

A message comes through the radio that I can't hear. I turn up the volume, but it doesn't help because he comes back inside yelling, "Look at those guys. Oh, man, I love that stuff."

"Curt, pipe down." I turn up the volume some more, but by then, the person has stopped talking.

He slumps back onto the chair and chuckles. "Oh yeah, those guys will tell everybody I'm on this boat. That's too cool." He jumps up, heads for the stairs, and disappears for the rest of the day.

With good fishing, by 0300 we can't fit another fish in our hold. I write detailed instructions in the watch book for Johnny and Bob, both trained seamen, to take the watch. I assign them two-and-a-half hours each, so I can hit my bunk for a much-needed break. Leaving the captain's chair, I know the boat is in good hands.

Minutes later it seems, I'm startled awake by a thumping bass and screaming guitar. In a foul mood, I ascend the four steps to the wheelhouse where Curt is kicked back in the driver's chair, feet up, yapping on the radio. I turn off the stereo, narrow my eyes at him, and slide a finger across my throat to cut the radio chatter.

He gives me a wide grin as he hangs up the microphone. "Hey, Capt, good nap?"

"Morning, Curt. Where're the boys?" I ask in a tone of disapproval.

"I told them I'd take the watch. I'm not tired," he replies as if I'd asked his favorite color.

My hands ball into fists. "I left instructions to wake me at 0800, and it's 0930."

"Yeah, I saw that in the watch book, but I figured I'd let you sleep. We still have eight hours before we get to the dock."

Fighting to control my anger, I manage to say in a level voice, "Get up, Curt. I'll take over." I approach the chair, surrounded by empty soda cans, candy wrappers, and an open can of chewing tobacco.

"Hold it." I sweep the garbage into his arms and grab the Dust Buster from the wall, sucking up crumbs and a pile of stinky Copenhagen. "Curt, you haven't been cleared to take a watch. I make sure a guy is trained first. Our lives depend on it."

"Oh, I know but—"

"And no one—not you, not even God—alters the watch schedule or neglects to wake me."

"I thought I was doing you a favor."

The disc of chewing tobacco pops from his grasp. The lid flies off as the can rolls across the carpet, leaving a filthy brown trail. "Dang, that stuff is expensive," Curt laments. "Uh, hey, Capt, guess I need your vacuum."

"You didn't even have permission to be on watch. You pull something like this again, you're gone."

Curt reaches for the vacuum in my hand, like I haven't just threatened to fire him, and I pull it out of reach.

"I'm not done. If I hear music in my room, it's too loud. Next time, I'll pull the plug permanently."

"Yeah, okay," Curt stares at his feet and the tobacco trail.

"Another thing: chatting on the radio is forbidden. Do not touch the radios. If you hear an S.O.S., you find me. We do things our own way. We're not like other boats you've worked on. Got it?"

With his arms full of trash, he looks at me with a slight grin. "Sure, Captain. Whatever you say. Can I vacuum now?"

As the weeks pass, Curt avoids me in the wheelhouse. He works hard, but he dominates the crew in most conversations and on work projects. When I enter the crew's area, he keeps his head down and looks busy.

After a trip of poor fishing, on the way back to port, I'm weary from fighting a storm. I bring the boat close to the dock, gripping the wheel and throttle in gale force winds, which requires steady concentration. My eyes feel like sandpaper.

The phone rings. I reluctantly release one hand from steering to answer.

"Hey, Jack. Everything okay?" It's Tom, my manager. He rarely calls.

"Uh...we had a tough trip." A heavy gust careens the boat straight for the dock. "Hey, Tom, I'm about to tie up," I say, struggling to keep my voice calm. "Can I call you back?"

"No, sorry. I'm boarding a plane, and you should hear this."

I jam the controls in reverse to avoid a crash. "What's up?"

"I got another email from Curt."

The boat shudders backing up. "*Another* one? Why is Curt emailing you?"

"He says you're harassing him and abusing the crew."

"What?"

"Says he's doing all the work."

Another strong gust heaves the boat toward the dock. I barely clear a rusty corner of broken concrete and steel. Throwing the boat into full reverse, the dock shrinks with the distance.

"You believe this guy?" I say, trying to keep the stress of the weather and Curt's idiocy from my voice.

"Jack, I've known you twenty-five years, and I've never heard anything like this under your command."

"Yeah, Okay. Curt has to go." I jog the steering, reversing and advancing to battle the winds—just another day.

Tom laughs. "Be careful. 'Abuse' and 'harass' are trigger words. He may be armed for a fight."

"I got his number, Tom. Thanks."

I shove the throttle forward, making no attempt to hide my fury, and swing the 123-foot vessel against the dock. The crew ties up as I call to the lower deck on the loud hailer: "Curt, come up here, please."

Seconds later, he sticks his head in the door and says, "Hey, Capt, what's up?"

"Step inside and close the door," I reply from the other side of the wheelhouse.

"I hoped to see Pauly..." Winds swirl into the wheelhouse as he stands in the open doorway.

"Sit down, Curt." I slam the door on my side of the wheelhouse. "Do you know why I called you up here?"

A big smile creases his face as he sits in the portside chair, closest to the door he entered. "Yeah. You're giving me a raise."

"How's that?"

"I do everything on here."

"Yes. You've tried to take over every position, including mine."

"Well, yeah. I make sure things get done because no one listens to me."

"And why do you think that is?" I walk to the chart table, six feet from him.

"They're jealous because I'm going to be a captain someday."

"They're not jealous. No one wants to work with you. You're finished here."

His arrogant smirk vanishes, and his eyes go wide. "What?"

"You're fired, Curt. I'll have a plane ticket for you in an hour."

"Wait. No way. I can't be fired."

"You can't imagine how fired you are."

"Hold on. I don't get it."

"You're fired *because* you don't get it."

He explodes from his chair. "This is a bunch of crap. I'm calling Tom."

"Tom knows I'm letting you go. He called to tell me about your emails."

"This is ridiculous," Curt yells and stomps down the stairs toward the galley. "You guys are hopeless without me."

I spot Bobby, the deck boss, outside my door, and make a hand signal to round up the crew and come inside. The crew meets me in the galley, still dressed in heavy coats and hats. They sit quietly at the table, their eyes avoiding their shipmate who's pacing on the opposite side of the room.

"I'm getting a lawyer," Curt mumbles.

"Curt is leaving," I tell the other four men. "Help him get his stuff." I look at Curt. "How you depart will show if you're a professional or not."

Later that day, heading back out to sea, the crew smiles on deck and I hear laughter, things I haven't seen for some time.

COURAGE

Being a captain of a boat, a CEO, a supervisor, a teacher, a team leader,
or any other person in a position of authority doesn't make a leader.
An effective leader can't be a coward, yet dealing with egos can take
diplomacy. Still, sometimes diplomacy doesn't work. Then the leader has
to stand up to that strong personality to improve the environment for
everyone. In my case, being Captain Jack meant it was my boat
and my crew. My job was to protect them both.

Taking Charge

My stomach lurches in the turbulent skies as the Boeing 737 drops into Nome Alaska. Rain slashes my window, and I pull my seat belt tighter. The plane banks violently sideways. Babies scream, and a can of soda rolls in the aisle.

"Please, hang on as we prepare..." is all the pilot's voice manages on the intercom. The plane's descent leaves me weightless just before we hit the runway—hard. The tires howl, the wings flex, and the plane jolts forward, slamming me against my belt. We rock and shake as the brakes shudder the floor under my feet, slowing the plane enough to taxi to the hanger.

At the open door of the aircraft, freezing rain stings my face. I bend at the waist and run across the tarmac. Ice water soaks through my clothes and slides down my back. The rusty double doors at the hanger won't open more than a couple feet, so I wait in line to enter single-file with the other passengers. Without a rain gutter at the edge of the roof, water cascades onto our heads. I help an elderly Alaskan couple and a single mom with two crying kids get out of the storm before I enter.

In the waiting area, I shake my wet head and spot my deck boss from the Norseman II. Billy, dressed in full orange rain gear and rubber boots, stands out in the denim and Carhartt crowd.

"How's things?" I ask, shaking his hand.

"We're all glad you made it, Captain Jack," he says. "If you didn't, we'd have to sail with Charles again."

"I'm sure glad for that pilot. The flight was insane," I say to diffuse Billy's comment.

I've returned to Nome after a six-week break. I'll resume my position as captain on the Norseman II, a 115-foot research vessel.

Charles has been captain in my absence. I'm experienced using trawl gear, a skill the scientists require this trip into the Arctic oceans. Charles agreed to step down as captain and be my first mate.

A teeth-rattling screech of metal against metal signals the opening of a bent, rusty door above the luggage ramp. Cold wind sweeps through the passenger area as bags, palates of food, dog kennels, and backpacks tumble down the sloped sheet metal for the locals returning home from Anchorage. When my sodden bag appears, I swing the strap on my shoulder, and Billy and I make our way through the tight crowd.

Opening the door to the outside, biting Arctic water pours off the roof and douses our heads. Billy and I do our best to skirt the puddles, but my pants are still coated in mud by the time we arrive at the rental truck. Once we get on the road, I shout over the thundering exhaust, due to the missing muffler, "So, Billy, what's going on? What do I need to know?"

Squinting to see through the only clear spot on the windshield from a single wiper blade, he says, "We're ready to go after the scientists pick up a few boxes from this flight."

"Great. How'd you do breaking in a new captain?"

"Well, like I said, everyone is glad you're coming." Billy's lips twitch in a slight smile.

"C'mon, Billy. I want to know what I'm walking into."

"Charles don't know much, and he won't listen to anybody. You're the opposite—you always listen, and you know what the hell you're doing."

"Okay, well, he's a mate now. We should be able to handle that, huh?"

"Yeah, Captain," he agrees with another smirk.

We arrive next to the dock. The Norseman II surges on the sea swells as the Nome harbor provides little protection for big boats. Stepping out of the truck, my rain-saturated shirt and muddy pants cling to me. Billy grabs my bag as I jump the rail and climb the steps to the wheelhouse. The deck looks clean, all the equipment in place.

Billy sets my bag inside the door, gives me a wary glance, and disappears. A short muscular guy, whom I assume is Charles, talks on a cell phone by the chart table as if I'm not here. His body reminds me of a beer keg, round and stalky. He's about five-foot-six, has a shiny bald head and a strong jaw. Dressed in pressed jeans, a gray fisherman's sweater, and bright white sneakers, his clothes look like he just got back from the Anchorage shopping mall.

I glance around to see the wheelhouse is well-organized and spotless—except for the muddy puddle that has formed at my feet by the time Charles ends his conversation. His gaze drops to my soggy shoes on the carpet with the annoyance of someone whose space has been invaded. I toss a friendly wave, grab my bag, and walk toward him.

"You must be Charles. Good to meet you." I extend my hand. "I have to get out of these clothes, so I'll be back up in a bit." His fingers feel like limp, fat sausages.

"Take your time, Jack. I got everything under control up here."

I'd think he was being nice if he didn't cross his arms, and my back didn't prickle with his stare as I walk to the captain's stateroom.

When I get to my room for the next two months, the bed is expertly made, but Charles hasn't moved out his many bags yet. Needing the floor space to change my clothes, I open the door and set his gear in the hallway. When I'm dressed in dry jeans and a clean sweater, I notice the bags are gone on my way back to the wheelhouse.

I walk upstairs to see Charles instructing two of the crew outside the door on the upper deck. The crewman closest to me is PJ, a good kid I've worked with plenty. His face lights up when he sees me, so I step outside the wheelhouse to greet him.

When PJ starts toward me, Charles barks, "PJ, I'm not done talking."

I put up a finger, nod for PJ to wait, and go back inside to check the instruments, the charts, and our intended assignment. Charles returns to the wheelhouse. Seeing me studying the charts, he grabs a clipboard at the corner of the chart table.

"Jack, I'll take care of everything," he says, staring at his clipboard. "All you have to worry about is towing the nets."

"What's left to do before we can get out of here?" I ask, figuring I'll deal with his ego later. The charter requires a skipper with five years' experience towing fishnets, and Charles has none.

"The last of the scientific equipment is coming on now. I've already had an orientation meeting with the crew and guests, so we can sail in thirty minutes.

As captain, I should be present at the orientation, so I say, "Okay, Charles. Please spread word that I want everyone to gather in fifteen minutes in the conference room."

His head snaps sideways to really look at me for the first time. "I've already covered everything."

"I have no doubt you have." I walk to the door. "Never mind. I'll get the word out myself and have a look around."

Without waiting for a response, I leave the wheelhouse. Seeing both familiar and new faces on my walk through the boat, I'm met with smiles and handshakes all around. After I've invited everyone to orientation, I stand at the front of the wood paneled room and greet everyone as they enter. When all twenty guests are seated in chairs at the large conference table, and our eight crew members have convened in the back of the room, I begin.

"Welcome aboard. I'm Captain Jack. I see lots of people I know and am looking forward to meeting those of you I don't know. I've commanded boats in these northern waters for almost thirty years, and so far, everyone has come back alive."

The crowd chuckles.

"This is my fourth year bringing the Norseman II into the ice.

She's a fine vessel, and the crew is experienced. We will do every-thing we can to accommodate your needs to insure the best possible data for your experiments. I want to emphasize the importance of airing little problems before they become big ones. Thirty souls in tight quarters for three weeks can be a stretch for anyone. My door is always open, and I'll listen. We have everything going for us, so let's head up to the Arctic Circle and get to work."

After my introduction, I return to the wheelhouse where Charles hands me another clipboard. "I have the watch schedule for the next two days," he informs me.

Without looking at it, I toss the schedule on the chart table, slap my hands together with glee and say, "Let's get this show on the road."

Pulling away from the dock, I hang my head out a side window and hear PJ laughing, saying, "Oh, man. It's so easy with Jack here."

"Hey, PJ, you getting weak on me?" I tease.

"No, Capt. It's just great to have you back."

"Yeah, well, that's the goal: make it look easy, right?"

"Aye, aye, Capt."

The clouds have cleared, and the sun is still high in the Arc-tic summer sky at ten o'clock in the evening. Weary from the long flight, I sit in a wheelhouse chair, filling out the ship's log, letting the sun warm me through the windows. After securing the scientific equipment and arranging pallets of gear with the crane, PJ comes up for a visit.

"Hey, what's with all the logbooks and clipboards?" I ask him.

"Ha, Capt, that's Charles." PJ laughs. "On watch, he makes us scribble everything on a clipboard with a pencil and then enter the information with a pen in a what he calls a 'dirty log.' Then, only he can make his perfect entries in the ship's log. This guy is OCD to the max."

After two days of fine sailing, the vessel reaches the edge of the Arctic ice cap in the Chukchi Sea. The morning dawns sunny and beautiful, the air fresh, the sea reflecting azure skies as ice chunks lazily float past us. The crew deploys and retrieves scientific instruments from the pristine waters of the Arctic Sea. We quickly find a rhythm between myself controlling the big boat and the crew swinging on and off the expensive equipment.

A grinning Billy visits the wheelhouse during a short break and says, "Jack, we got more done this morning than we would have all day with Charles, and we're not working half as hard."

I take a swig of coffee and set the cup in the holder near the radar screen. "Cut the guy a break. I got a lot of years doing this. Running a boat isn't something you learn overnight."

"Well, whatever, boss. There's a lot of happy campers on deck. The scientists are adding more work because we're flying through the assignments."

"Yeah, okay. We're having fun, but let's not get cocky. You're only as good as your last move, right?"

He chuckles. "You've always said that, Capt."

A happy crew is a direct reflection of leadership, and my goal is to have things run smoothly, whether fishing or helping scientists collect data to study the sea and its creatures.

That evening, Charles arrives in the wheelhouse, five minutes before he's to take over the night shift. I haven't seen him all day. He picks up the ship's log, scowls at my recent entries, and stares out the window at the ocean ahead.

"Hey, I understand you've run over quite a few buoys. If you'd like, I can help you with that," I offer. "I've trained quite a few guys how to handle a boat in tight quarters."

His head snaps sideways, and his eyes narrow at me. "That's not necessary. If the crew would do their job and finish on time, I wouldn't have to make a bad approach."

I grab the binoculars, looking at nothing on the horizon, and say, "It's the captain's job to pace the whole operation. If the crew doesn't finish on time, the captain needs to make adjustments. The way I play it, I'm the coach. The deck boss is the quarterback. I set the plays, and he executes them. We have to finish one play before starting the next."

"I'd never give the deck boss that much power. He needs to do what I say."

No wonder the crew hates him.

"Well, have a nice evening, Charles. Wake me if you have any questions."

With the sun still bright and the sea like glass, I stroll down to the back deck and stand behind a stack of equipment. As the boat advances to the next buoy, Billy says a little too loudly, "Oh crap. Anybody notice what time it is? I bet Charles is driving. Look at this stupid approach."

Billy throws the grappling hook, grabbing the next set of floats. "Slow down! Slow down, Charles!" he shouts so loud, I cringe. "Help me hold this, guys."

Two deck hands run to the rail to help hold the line attached to the hook, still out in the water. The boat shudders in full-power reverse, and the crew groans as the boat slides over the buoy, dragging the line under the hull. The guys are forced to release the line, and it snaps like a whip.

"Damn, that hurt." PJ shakes off his gloves and blows into his palms.

"Holy crap," Billy says. "What's with that guy? This didn't happen all day with Jack driving." He tramps to the forward wall, grabs the intercom, and calls the wheelhouse. "Yeah, Charles, we have to go back around. We lost that one under the boat." He listens for a few seconds and adds, "I grabbed the line as soon as I could, but you were going too fast and ran it over." Hanging up the phone, Billy looks at PJ and says, "Charles wants me in the wheelhouse."

I'm tempted to step in, but I decide to stay hidden behind the equipment and wait to see what happens.

Before Billy even reaches the wheelhouse, I hear Charles yelling. I can't make out what he says, but clearly, Billy's getting an ass-chewing. Seconds later, Billy stomps past my hiding place, kicking a bucket of soapy water that splashes under a life rail and tumbles overboard. Next, he kicks a coil of rope, unwinding it across the deck. I'll have to do something to diffuse the tension, or this trip could devolve into disaster.

The following morning, I purposely hang out at the galley coffee pot to see the day crew. "Okay, boys, the seas are rough today," I say as I fill my cup. "Looks like six-foot swells with a two-foot wind chop. I use a lot of sayings, and one is: 'When the seas pick up, we slow down.' We'll get through the scientists' assignments today, but we'll do it at a slow, steady pace. Let's make that the goal: no hurries, nice and smooth."

"You can't imagine how good that sounds, Capt," Billy says.

PJ sighs and nods.

"You're the deck boss. A good boat runs without drama." I pour another cup and hand it to Billy. "I'll give you all the time you need. We'll make it look easy."

The morning proceeds how I envisioned. I position the boat in the swells to make the least amount of motion on deck. Boat handling is critical. Being both careful and bold, we swing heavy, expensive scientific gear into the sea and retrieve it without a fuss. During a short break in the action, the intercom buzzes.

"Hey, boss, this is so cool," says Billy's voice through the speaker. "We're rocking it down here, just like you said."

"Yeah, good job, Billy. Tell the guys we're right on schedule."

Pulling up to the next set of buoys, the crew fails to throw the grapple hook. I call on the loudspeaker, "Hey, you guys there?" No one answers. "Billy, give me a call."

In seconds, my phone rings. "Hey, boss."

Standing up, looking out the back window, I see the buoys slip past the stern, out of reach. "Why aren't you throwing the hook?"

I hear someone shouting in the background and say, "What's going on?"

"Charles is here, Capt. He ordered us to shut down operations."

"He did what?" The guy's not arrogant enough to be that stupid—is he?

"He's out here telling us the sea conditions are too rough, and anyone on the boat can shut down the deck if they feel it's too dangerous. He says it's in the charter rules."

"Okay. Hang tight. Nobody is going anywhere."

Except, maybe Charles.

I grab my half-cup of cold coffee, gulp it down, and say to the empty wheelhouse, "He's calling me out, and he's about to lose."

I grab my hard hat and step onto the back deck, hands on hips. The four crew stand on the left, three scientists huddle around their sample tables on the right, and Charles stands in the middle. Everyone is dead silent, their eyes darting from me to Charles.

"Charles, follow me, please." I turn my back to everyone, yank down the lever to open the gear room door, and step inside the four-by five-foot space where the crew hang their deck suits and helmets. Hot and humid from a space heater, the air smells of sweat and rubber boots.

The spring-loaded door shuts behind me—without Charles. I look through the window to see he hasn't moved, so I reopen the heavy door with my shoulder. "Charles, you get your ass in here, or I'll have the crew deliver you."

Charles glances at the crew. Their faces are resolute, waiting for my command. Reluctantly, he moves forward and joins me in the cramped room. Before the door clicks shut, I light into him.

"I have no idea what you're doing, but I'm the captain. You're the mate. I know you don't like it, and I couldn't care less. As mate..." I poke my finger at his broad chest. "...you don't make a move without me knowing about it."

"Don't do this, Jack. Don't you dare do this." He sucks air through clenched teeth, and cords bulge in his neck.

"Don't do what?" I glare at him, daring him to defy me.

"You can't override my call on deck. It's too rough to work and you know it."

"Charles, you don't know squat. The sad thing is, you think you know it all, but you're a lousy boat driver. You're lucky I haven't replaced you with a deck hand and put you on the beach."

His eyes flare with anger. I get the feeling he might attack me. At the window, I put up an index finger for Billy to stand by and realize the whole crew is watching. Billy nods.

"If you continue to work in these dangerous conditions, I'll file a red card," Charles squawks close to tears. "I swear, I will. You'll be finished."

I almost laugh. "You can file a hundred red cards. I could give a rat's ass. From now on, you stay off that deck, and you leave my crew alone. If you try a stunt like this again, I'll have you zip-tied and stuffed into your room."

I let Charles open the door leading to the inside of the boat to storm off. At the stairway descending to his quarters, he stops and rages at full volume, "I'm filing a red card. You're toast, Captain Jack!"

The scientists at their workstations stare at me. Charles stomps down the steps and slams his door.

After a couple of deep breaths, I announce on the intercom, "Okay, everyone, the cook baked a fresh batch of cookies. Let's all take fifteen minutes and get back to work."

The scientists glance at one another, seemingly pleased. I go back out on deck to see the crew slapping high-fives and pumping fists.

"Man, he messed with our chi, Capt," says Billy, making the crew laugh and breaking the tension.

Altercations on a boat at sea are tough, nothing like being on land. The people who are at odds can't leave. What might feel like a big space at the start of a voyage shrinks as tensions rise. Everyone shares the same eating space, common areas, and operation of the vessel. Rumors and gossip run rampant.

I bring a load of cookies and hot coffee to the wheelhouse and call Jim, the vessel owner.

"Sorry, Jack. It sounds like you did the right thing," he says, "but I'm concerned about a red card."

Munching a cookie, I ask, "What's a red card? Charles swings it like an axe."

"It's what the industry looks at before they'll charter the boat, like a report card. The red card will affect our ability to get work in the future. Let's see if he's serious or bluffing. Can you still work with him? Stopping the trip would be a disaster."

"I'll make it work, but I'm not cutting this jerk any slack."

"I don't blame you. Good luck."

That night, Charles reports for watch on time. "Can you drive?" I ask.

"Yes," he answers softly without looking at me.

"You'll pilot this boat and nothing else. You won't speak to the crew unless there is an emergency. Is that clear?"

"Yes," he says quietly.

"We have nine days left. Let's get through this."

As I stroll below decks, PJ approaches me. "Capt I want you to know, Charles has a key to your room." PJ's eyes are wide with fear which says a lot. He's a brave kid.

"Okay, PJ. I appreciate it." Passing by the empty galley, I grab a red handled Victorinox knife. I balance the razor-sharp weapon, switching hands for practice, then pick up a few more cookies.

Before going to bed, I visit the wheelhouse, and Charles tenses in the captain's chair.

"Do you have a key to my room?" I ask.

His body jerks, startled. He grabs his clipboard, looking busy, and says, "No, there's a key in the medicine cabinet."

There's a key in the cabinet, like he said, but that doesn't mean he doesn't have one, so I take the knife to bed with me. Sleeping lightly, with the door locked and the knife under my pillow, I occasionally squeeze the cold nylon handle.

The following day, the onboard safety officer, Ron, who had been onboard the six weeks Charles was captain, tells me Charles submitted a red card. "Jack, I saw the whole thing on deck," Ron says. "I'm glad someone finally stood up to that jerk. I'll send in my own review. Charles is cooked. That card will never see the light of day."

Nine days later, back in Nome, Charles is first to step off the boat without saying goodbye to anyone. As far as I know, he's never worked on another boat.

I hear he's driving a cab in Anchorage.

FAITH

The Bible defines faith as "Faith shows the reality of what we hope for; it is the evidence of things we cannot see." (Heb 11:1).
A leader knows many things are beyond his or her control.
Control is an illusion. We can never truly control our world.
My wife and I released our son, having faith in people to help him get home. In the end, his safety depended on him and God. I rely on faith when things are out of my hands. It's okay. Belief is like that.

Alaska Grows Gus

"C'mon, Dad. Let's get off the boat," Gus, my eight-year-old pleads. After three months of hauling salmon on the 123-foot Columbia, walking on land will be a treat. It's low tide, and we're forced to climb twenty feet up a rickety ladder to reach the dock. We're greeted by busy workers driving forklifts, stacking big totes of Salmon. We take a shortcut, walking on weathered boards that keep us above the deep grass, wildflowers, and mud. The planks end as we come onto a one-lane dirt road, leaving the village of Larson Bay, Alaska behind us.

A four-wheeler blasts by. The native driver, wearing a black baseball cap backwards, spews clouds of dust in his wake. The mud-caked machine gets a hundred yards past us when the driver slams to a stop on a low wooden bridge, spins, and comes roaring back to us.

"There's a bear by the bridge, a big one!" he says with deep wrinkles creasing his smiling eyes and gaps in his wide grin. "Stay on the bridge, and you'll be okay. He swipes dust from his gray stubble. "I'm Peter. Have a good day." He cranks his machine around. Dirt billows behind him as rides back over the bridge.

This place is famous for grizzlies. I contemplate the bridge—gray, broken beams barley spanning the water, no guardrails. "Hey, Gus, you ready to see a bear?"

Gus grips my hand and looks up at me. "Is it safe, Dad?"

My wife and I took Gus out of school early to come north with me. Fishermen are absent from home a lot. Gus lives with his mom and two sisters most of the year. This past winter, while wrestling, Gus shouted at me: "My panties! You got my panties."

"What?" I let go of him, my arms collapsing at my sides. "What did you call them?"

"Panties. Why?"

"I'm taking you to Alaska." I look at my wife, Joanne, standing by the fire holding Kirdy, our youngest, in her arms. "He can hang with me and the guys."

The school district protested our pulling Gus from third grade a month early, and Joanne's friends said things like: "Aren't you afraid for his safety?" and "That's a lot of school to miss."

Gus squeezes my hand as we near the bridge. Next to the the road, the thick brush, ripe with berries, could be crawling with Kodiak bears. Nat-Geo films the largest bears in the world in this part of Alaska.

"We'll go slow." I lay my arm across Gus's shoulders. "Don't run. Bears are faster than you."

Gus stops. "We need a gun, Dad."

I squat, pushing his curly blonde hair from his fearful eyes, and pat his arm. "We'll just watch, Gus. We'll be okay."

Cautiously stepping onto the bridge, we scan the area. Nothing, no bear. Fifty feet beyond, to our left, the water forks with heavy brush on both sides. Salmon fight upstream to spawn. The only sound is the water gurgling over green rocks. The air smells of fresh cedar and moss. I guide my son with a hand on his back and he resists. "C'mon," I say. "Let's cross the bridge."

Thirty feet away, a brown furry streak the size of a Volkswagen, leaps from the brush. Gus jerks, ready to bolt. I grip the back of his neck. "Stand still, Gus. Don't move."

Splash! Whump! The grizzly pounces on a salmon in the stream. Gus squirms against my hand. I quietly crouch, whispering, "He doesn't see us. He's busy eating."

The grizzly sits with its back to us in shallow water. We see glimpses of the fat salmon shuddering between massive jaws. We're so close, we can hear the bear crunching and slurping.

Minutes pass and Peter returns on his four-wheeler, skidding to a stop. He climbs from his Yamaha and meets us on the bridge. "He's a big one. Bruno's getting fat for winter." He looks at Gus. "You like the bear?"

"Yeah," Gus whispers.

"It was pretty exciting to see him jump." I glance at my son.

"Oh yeah?" Peter turns and steps back to his machine, hitting the horn. Beep, beep!

The bear's nose goes up toward the sky. It roars, standing on its hind legs, spinning toward us, paws raised.

"Holy crap, Peter!" I yell and hold onto Gus.

Peter's shoulders jostle with laughter. "Bruno always does that. He won't leave his fish."

As quick as the bear rises, it drops back into the stream to finish its salmon.

"We better get back to the boat, Gus," I say and force a smile. "Thanks, Peter."

"Glad you had the opportunity to meet Bruno." Peter gives me a big grin and handshake.

Gus and I walk back to the bay front lined with hundred-year-old buildings. Built for salmon canning, the weathered gray walls and rusty metal roofs harken to another era. Tidy bunkhouses painted in yellows, blues, greens, and reds frame the dock. Whimsical signs like "Hen House" hang above the doors. Window pots burst with flowers. Rugged bicycles lean against the colorful buildings. College-age girls and boys sit together on benches by the water.

A bell jingles when I swing open the huge wooden door to the cannery office. Framed salmon can labels hang on the walls. The office manager, Betty, greets us, makes a fuss over Gus, and offers us donuts. A ten-year-old is rare here. I find Jerry, our busy manager, on the phone, and he waves us into his office. A mish-mash of papers and three phones clutter his desk, and a tall stack of nautical charts sit on a table against the wall.

Ending his call and hanging up, Jerry says, "Hi, Jack. Hey, Gus, how you doing, kid?" Shaking our hands, we each take a seat in big oak chairs in front of his chaotic desk.

I wink at Jerry. "We saw a bear at the bridge."

"Oh yeah? That's Bruno. He's there all summer."

I laugh and don't mention how frightened we were.

"I know you want to get home, but we'll need you another ten days, maybe two weeks," Jerry says, leaning back in his chair.

I purse my lips and exhale. "Okay, but I have to get Gus to school."

"What? Ahh, why do that?" Jerry smiles at Gus. "Aren't you having fun?"

"Yeah, I like it up here," Gus says shyly, staring at his lap.

"I'd keep him," I say, "but he missed the last month of third grade. We've gotten grief already."

"Ha, I bet you have." Jerry leans forward in his chair, propping his elbows on his thighs. "What could be better for a boy than a summer in Alaska with his dad?"

I toss up a hand. "My thoughts exactly."

"Can you get going by noon tomorrow?" he asks.

"Sure. I'll work something out." I look at Gus, missing him already.

"A bush plane comes through in the morning. It could drop Gus in Kodiak," Jerry offers.

"I'll make some calls," I say. "Thanks."

His phone rings, and we bow out of his office. I grab a free phone and call Joanne while Gus sits near Betty in the front office. "Honey, the company needs our boat here longer than I thought."

"How will you get Gus home from such a remote place?" she says with panic in her voice. "People already think I'm nuts for letting him go so long."

I sigh with the weight of family clashing with work. "Sweetheart, our eight-year-old will hop a bush plane to Kodiak, fly a jet to Anchorage, board the red-eye to Seattle, then switch planes to Portland."

After a short silence, she says, "Oh, no, please. Isn't there another way?"

"I know I told you I would put him on a plane myself, but I have to ship out tomorrow by noon. I'll ask around. Maybe someone can help."

"I'm sure he's grown up this summer, but he's only eight." She exhales into the phone. "I'll pray for you both."

Walking back to the boat, Gus's brows wrinkle and he asks, "What's going to happen to me, Dad?"

Crouching on the dock to look him in the eyes I say, "We'll figure this out, bud. I promise."

On the boat, I gather the crew on the back deck. "Hey, guys, we'll be here ten more days, maybe two weeks. Any questions?"

Hans, a German, speaks up. "Ya, Captain. My brother has a spot open on a crabber in Dutch Harbor." The sun illuminates his brilliant white skin. The tattoos from his former years as a skinhead are blacked out on his arms.

"How soon, Hans?"

"Sooner the better."

"Okay, let me get back to you."

Gus jumps into my bunk to play video games while I go to the wheelhouse and make coffee, asking myself: if Hans leaves, could he take Gus with him through the airports? He's a good worker, but can I trust him with my son?

I call Hans to the wheelhouse. "You have a real opportunity," I tell him. "I know those guys in Dutch. Between leaving here and going there, though, you can really blow it. I've seen guys do it."

"Blow it, Captain?"

"Guys get hammered, miss their planes, and lose their jobs. Are you going to start drinking as soon as you hit the airport?"

"I did that kinda stuff a few years ago, but I gave that up."

"Don't try to fool me, Hans. I'll find out."

"Ah, yeah. No drinking. I want that job bad."

"Okay, then I need to ask a favor." I've been fooled before, but I don't see another option. "Can you take Gus to Anchorage with you and make sure he gets on his plane to Seattle?"

"Sure, Captain. I'll do that."

I look hard at him. "Hans, this is not easy to send my son with anyone besides myself, so know this: if anything goes bad, I will find you."

"I like your boy. He'll be safe with me."

"Thanks, Hans. Okay, I'll make arrangements."

The past three months with Gus have been sweet. He loves boat life, the fishermen, big catches, bears, and whales. Early seasickness and helping him brave through storms seem like nothing compared to letting him go.

The morning is sunny, and the bay reflects the sapphire sky. I toss duffle bags into the skiff and squat to talk on Gus's level. "Remember the bear? You were scared, but it turned out pretty cool. There's nothing to be afraid of. You'll be home by this evening." I wrap my arms around him. "Okay, little man, you've done great. I'll see you at home soon."

I shake hands with Hans and repeat for the third time, "Keep him safe."

"Aye, aye, Captain." Hans playfully salutes with two fingers at his forehead, his head freshly shaven.

The skiff races away to the float plane, and my stomach twists with anxiety.

That night, I get a call from my wife. "Well, Gus made it to Seattle," she says. "But he sat alone in the Anchorage airport for five hours. Hans left in a taxi, said he had to buy a pair of Air Jordans and never returned."

The summer held many challenges for Gus. He dealt with puking over the side of the boat, working all night, and a crew who cut him no slack. Connecting through airports on his own is something he would not have had the courage to do before spending time on the Columbia.

Months later, I heard Hans never showed up for the new job. In fact, he was never seen again in the Bering Sea.

TEAMWORK

A pair of eagles in perfect harmony, pure synchronicity, controlled a chaotic scene. They exemplified focus and determination, expending only the energy needed to accomplish their task.

We can learn a lot from the eagles.

A Brush With Primal Fear

Savoring a rare, calm, storm-free day near Dutch Harbor, Alaska, I'm alone on the beach. The air smells of summer Aleutian grass and seaweed at low tide. The bay reflects the surrounding mountains, their volcanic cones highlighted with patches of snow. As captain of the Columbia, I'm rarely able to get off the boat.

Just when I think this day can't get any better, sunlight breaks through puffy scattered clouds, casting perfect light for a photograph on the two bald eagles, perched near the grass where the rocks meet the water.

The eagles sit apart. I can't frame them both in my lens, so I choose the largest of the two, probably a female, and focus on her. If I can get closer, I'll get a better shot, so I start to move forward. My rubber boots slip on the wet smooth boulders as salt water surges around the rocks and gravel. I have to keep one eye on my feet to maneuver without falling.

I stop to adjust the settings on my full-frame camera and check the exposure. The female hasn't moved, but her head comes up, stretching her neck. Her head pivots to the left, then the right. Other than the rise and fall of the sea, the air is silent. I peer through my camera lens and watch her neck slowly relax as she resumes her regal pose.

I'm still too far away to get a decent shot, so I advance cautiously again, holding my backpack in one hand, my camera in the other, hoping I'll seem smaller to the eagles without my pack on my back. On a large boulder, I carefully sit and swing my legs around, soaking my butt. Glancing up occasionally, keeping eye contact with the birds to a minimum, I breathe deep and long, feeling alive in such a beautiful moment.

Then a blood curdling screech rips through my peace and makes my hair stand up. Out of reflex, I raise my camera. The big female lunges directly at me at lightning speed, her head down, wings pumping. She's low to the ground, at eye level.

"Get the shot, Jack. Get the shot," is all I can think. I frame the seven-foot wingspan and mash the shutter button. She charges so fast, shooting five frames per second, I only manage four before I have to duck, raising an elbow with the camera pack over my head. Her high-pitched cry sounds ear piercingly close, and I feel a whoosh of air from her wings.

I brace for impact, wishing I'd worn my hat.

Her massive shape careens overhead, stabbing through the space where my head had been. I snatch a glimpse of her tail and immense wingspan as she passes me.

"Whew! Wow!" I whisper. "Glad she missed."

Another deadly screech emanates at the right of me. Still crouched on the boulder, I spin, looking for the source. Cloaked by the sun, the male eagle dives at me. In shock, I drop my camera and dive to the wet gravel between boulders, curling in a fetal position with freezing seawater soaking into my side, my heart banging inside my ribcage.

I peek between my elbows to see the male hovering for a few colossal wing beats. His eyes are angry, his screech never falters, and his commanding face gives me an unforgettable rebuke, immobilizing me with fright.

The male joins his mate in the air. The eagles fly opposite one another, squawking in unison in a perfect orbit above me. Their ear-splitting chides and unwavering, confrontational gazes terrorize me. I feel confused, even foolish as I huddle in the wet gravel, under attack by wild animals. I've never been threatened like this, though I've photographed eagles for years.

Shivering and stiff from being jammed between the rocks for

several minutes, I realize the sentries in the sky don't plan to leave, so I gather my sand-covered camera and put it in my bag as nonchalantly as I can, my hands shaking only a little. I study the big birds, masters of the sky, and decide their circular flight pattern and constant screeching, though scary, hasn't changed. Without rising, I squirm in the wet gravel to shimmy my arms into the straps on my backpack and say to myself, "You're not hurt. You have good legs, so get up and run."

With both birds in view, I roll into a pushup position. Their screeches pick up in cadence and intensify. Crap.

"Now or never, Jack," I tell myself and bring my feet under me into a crouch again. I scope out a path to escape through the boulders and launch like a hundred-meter sprinter.

An eagle instantly rolls and dives, screaming terrifying threats. Coming directly behind me, I first hear, then feel, the raptor come within inches of my head. I duck and keep running, sliding and catching myself, over and over, on the slick, wet rocks.

Another assault comes from behind, and again I feel a close swoop and screech. With both arms over my head, I slip on kelp, crashing my side into a boulder. The pain of impact sears through my body. Shock and fear overwhelm me. Dismayed and disoriented, I lay on my back across a flat boulder looking up.

The female comes at me again on my left, but I can't run. Instinctively, I roll off the boulder. I have to move, so I stumble and plod in survival mode, disengaged from logic. I cling to my ribs, bent sideways, unable to raise my arms.

The eagles halt their attack as soon as I reach the deep grass, near my truck. I scramble up the hill, dive into the driver's side, and double-check the windows. The pair have returned to the perch where I'd first spotted them, but from this elevated angle, I can see two young chicks are hiding in the grass.

So, that's it. I crack a water bottle, trying to collect my thoughts.

The eagles perfectly orchestrated their defense against me, an intruder. They clearly told me: "That's far enough." With masterful skills, the pair confused me and used my fear to assure every swoop pushed me further from their offspring.

After my adrenalin and emotions settle, I realize their strategy was never intended to harm me. If they'd wanted to hurt me, I'd have scars. Theirs was an escalation of power to prevent me from getting closer.

Humans are conditioned to everyday dangers. We've all suffered the loss of loved ones due to auto accidents, cancers, and myriad other misfortunes. However, we don't consider being eaten or ripped apart by a wild animal.

Nature's beasts obey instincts, and I had no way to convince the eagles I was harmless. My life was not in danger, but my survival mode sure kicked in. It's an unfamiliar and sobering thing, to be attacked by creatures with their own set of rules.

But I did get one amazing shot.

GRATEFULNESS

We're not *independent, though sometimes we'd like to think we are. Success on almost any project or in any field comes from the efforts of many people. A leader is one cog in a set of gears.*

I questioned guys I trained over the years, "What sort of business are you in?"

With a puzzled look, they always answered, "The fishing business."

"No, you're in the people business," I'd say. "Without people, you'll never catch a fish, never get unloaded, never buy fuel, get repairs, or paid. The success you want can only come from all the people involved. Treat them well, and you will be rewarded."

Life At Sea

At age thirteen, my mom walked me onto the train in Sacramento, California. "Say, 'Hi' to Grandma and Grandpa and my sister," she said and gave me a quick kiss.

At Union Station in Portland, I found my grandparents waiting for me. Grandpa shook my hand as Grandma said, "You'd like to worry me sick, Jack Molan." Then she smothered me in hugs.

From the train station, they took me to a Greyhound bound for Seaside, Oregon. In two hours, I got off the bus and inhaled the salt air. My pulse picked up in anticipation. Soon I would see what I came for.

My auntie pulled to the curb in a huge Pontiac LeMans. "Oh, I'm so glad you came to stay with us," she said, but I didn't plan to spend much time at her house. Each day, on her way to work, she'd drop me with a sack lunch at my true destination. I'd come to hang out at the south end of Seaside, at the cove where I could watch the surfers ride the waves.

I stood on a boulder the size of a small car, spellbound, after hiking a mile over slick, smooth rocks to Second Point. Spindrift blew off waves two stories high that roared past me like locomotives. The white water exploded like bombs going off, the rocky shoreline rumbling under my feet. Smooth, gray faces pitched in perfect peeling curls. I knew this place would someday either give me the ride of my life or a horrible drowning.

Ancient spruce and fir trees formed a lush green wall behind me. Brilliant white seagulls skimmed the water's surface, not for food but to play in the rainbow of refracted light in the spray, outrunning the thundering breakers. The pulsing ocean both frightened and thrilled me.

"I'll be a surfer and live by the ocean," I swore on the rock that day.

By the time I graduated from high school, our family had moved to Tacoma Washington. I left my home in Tacoma at seventeen and moved to Seaside, Oregon. Initially, I flopped on Auntie's couch but quickly landed a restaurant job. Within a few weeks, I bought a Mercury Comet for a hundred bucks and rented a room in a small beach house with a couple of surfers. A job came up at a fish cannery, so I left the restaurant to work on a clean-up crew.

The slimy, smelly job paid better than dish washing, but the night shift is what I valued most. When I got off work, I could jump in my Comet and go hit the waves. I never once considered college. "I can go to school if there's something I want to learn," I would say when people asked about my plans for the future.

At the cannery dock one day, I helped offload a shrimp boat, breaking up the ice and scooping out pink crustaceans with my white plastic shovel. Buzz, a deck hand, sat nearby on a wooden crate against the railing, smoking his Camel non-filters and bragged: "I made twelve hundred bucks this week."

"What?" I stopped shoveling and squinted into the sun at him. "You made that much in a week?"

"Oh, yeah. It's been rocking. I'll bank thirty grand by the end of the season." He took a long drag on his cancer stick. "I just have to stay out of the bar."

I'd busted my butt working overtime that week and earned a quarter of what he made in three days. "So, Buzz, what do you do all winter?"

"Ah, the guys with families fish dungy crabs, but I go to Mexico—six months on, six months off."

I leaned on my shovel, dumbfounded. I'd just found the brass ring. Money and time—time and money. I wanted both. That summer, I turned twenty-one and decided my next job would be on a fishing boat.

When the surf was flat, I walked the docks looking for an opening. One day, I met a captain whose boat reflected his pride. The decks smelled of bleach from a recent wash-down. The lines were coiled and stored, the nets stacked neatly, and the fishing gear organized. His crew was painting deck boards, joking and laughing as they worked. I knew this boat had a reputation as a top producer and was thrilled the captain would talk to me.

"We don't need anyone. I've had the same guys for years." The captain pointed across the marina to a derelict scow that had rust stains running down the side of the hull, paint peeling off the wheelhouse, and a crew in filthy clothes. "That pile of crap is looking for help, but be careful, kid. I know you're hungry for work, but don't do it. Good boats rarely need help, and bad boats always need help. That boat is a widow maker."

His advice probably saved my life, more than once. I still quote him when young people on the docks ask me about work.

Later that summer, my big break came. I got hired on Pegasus, a brand-new shrimp trawler. The shiny blue hull and spotless gray decks made the boat a real standout—queen of the Astoria fleet. As a greenhorn, I made less, but I couldn't care less. I had a job on an awesome new boat.

I worked hard, jumping to do things the out-of-shape deck boss avoided. At twice my age, he'd been passed over as skipper. He felt he should be in the wheelhouse, not on deck, and sometimes he took out his frustration on me. I ran up ladders and crawled out in the rigging to untangle knotted lines. I hopped in the hold and waded through waist-deep ice, stacking fish. Nothing stopped me. I asked endless questions about nets, cable rigging, diesel engines, the shrimp we were catching, the weather, other boats, and how to navigate. The grizzled deck boss started calling me "Grasshopper", referring to the character who always asked the master questions in "Kung Fu", a popular TV show at the time—and the nickname stuck.

That fall, when fishing season ended, a rusty Chevy Impala, stacked with new bright orange, red, and yellow Lightning Bolt surfboards from Hawaii, pulled into the surfers' parking lot. I met the owner, David, who had a wide grin and an infectious laugh. At the campfire that evening, long after the others had left, David and I sat on a big driftwood log, still in our wetsuits, and I marveled at his tales of king crab fishing in the Bering Sea.

"We don't sleep, and the weather is insane. Boats stacked high with crab pots roll over, and big waves punch in their windows. If you live, you make big bucks," he told me. "I'm leaving to surf in France in a few days. In January, I gotta be back in Seattle to fly to Alaska to fish on the Royal Viking. The crew made a hundred ten grand on deck last year."

And I thought: I could buy a house in Seaside for forty-thousand.

When spring came, I saw David in a local restaurant. "Hey, you want to come see my new house?" he asked with that giant grin of his.

I followed him through deep green rainforest where big older homes dot the coastline. David had bought five acres on the Tillamook Head sea cliffs, overlooking the best surf spot in Oregon.

"I take off for Dutch Harbor, Alaska in a few days," he said, gazing out at the ocean. "Should only take a couple years to pay this off."

"Take me king crabbing," I said. "I'm ready anytime."

David laughed. "You can try Seattle, but no one I know is quitting or hiring."

I was determined to land a job on a king crab boat. My chances may have been slim, but I paid eight-hundred dollars for a '66 VW Bus and took many two-hundred-mile trips from Seaside to Ballard, near Seattle, Washington, where the Alaska crab fleet docked in the offseason. Sleeping in my bus at night, I spent the daylight hours walking the docks, using all the charm and energy I could muster to get a job, but no one would talk to me.

One evening, after a long day shoveling shrimp on the Pegasus,

I stopped by my auntie's for spaghetti dinner. "Oh, honey, some guy named David called," she said as she passed the salad bowl. "He sounds like a fun guy. He left his number."

I sprang from the table and grabbed the phone.

"Hey, Jack, I just got a job on a new 123-foot Marco king crab boat, so new, it's not even built yet, and I'll be captain," David told me. "It's named Columbia."

"Oh, wow," I said. "That's awesome!"

"You told me you wanted to go king crabbing. Were you serious?"

I swallowed hard. "Ah, yeah, absolutely!"

"You need a day or two to think about it?"

"I just thought about it. I'll go."

He chuckled. "Good. You're my only greenhorn. You'll make less money, but you can work up to full share."

I was so stoked, I'd have gone for free.

Joanne and I had fallen in love, but I needed a real job before I could marry her. "He's a surfer and a fisherman," she'd tell her friends. One calm evening as we walked the docks she told me, "Fishing is an honorable way to make a living." And she had my heart.

My Scandinavian beauty has a strong adventurous spirit, and she looked forward to the fisherman's life. After my first king crab season, we were married. I had just turned twenty-five, and she was twenty-six.

Joanne loved to come to Alaska with me. We spent months on the Columbia exploring much of the state waters, chasing salmon runs. She cooked for a small crew and took watches. Each summer, we'd venture together, taking in the beauty and magnificence of the Alaskan coastline in a storybook romance.

After three years, many thought Joanne would choose to stay home when our son arrived. "Having a kid isn't going to slow me down," she would tell people.

The next summer, she stepped off the plane and strolled over the gravel walkway in Dutch Harbor with our eight-month-old strapped to her back. Aboard the Columbia, our son traveled up and down the inside passage as well as crossed the Bering Sea and northern Pacific Ocean. To prepare meals in the galley, Joanne carried Gustav in his baby backpack. Gus's favorite game was to be put in the walker, hold up his hands, and giggle with joy as he scooted across the room, banging into walls as the boat rolled. The salmon fishing fleet learned we had a baby onboard, and soon we had fishermen coming to hang out with us and our little boy.

But in the next few years, we had two little girls as well. Joanne decided to stay home with our children in Cannon Beach, Oregon. We had a home built there that her father designed, using cash along the way to pay for materials and labor.

Seven years after David hired me, I became captain of the Columbia. I knew I was made for the position, but the job required me to be away from home for ten months of the year. After so many months away, I worried our son and two younger daughters wouldn't remember who I was. The thought tore me up. I was good at my job, but I had to prioritize my family.

Gratefully, the boat owners and managers arranged for me to rotate with another captain. I worked two months on and two months off. My original idea to fish, make a good living, and have time off became a reality.

When Gus, our oldest, was eight years old, Joanne and I decided he needed more time with me. Toward the end of third grade, we pulled him from school, so I could take him to Alaska. The school district and some of Joanne's friends thought we were crazy. "What better thing could a boy do than be with his dad?" Joanne would ask.

Gus was a natural. He loved everything about the fishing life. He learned navigation using paper and electronic charts. He hung with the crew splicing lines and mending nets. He helped scrub the deck, including scraping and painting the bleeding rust. Keeping track of other boats' movements with me intrigued him. Watching whales and sea-lions thrilled him. Catching huge numbers of fish excited him. He enjoyed everything about those first four months, and every summer afterwards, he begged me to take him to the Bering Sea.

When our daughters were younger, Joanne sent them to cousins' houses in California. The girls bonded with their relatives while Joanne ventured north for a few weeks in the summers, cooking for the crew and spending time on the Columbia with Gus and me.

At thirteen, Gus began gill-netting salmon in Bristol Bay and continued throughout his high school years. When Gus went off to college, he felt trapped and emailed: "Dad, I seriously don't know what I'm doing here. I just talked to one of my professors, and I make more money than he does."

I wrote back: "Son, the option to return to fishing is always open. Try to hang in there and finish college."

Gus did graduate from college. He even got a job on land—and only lasted six months. Gus returned to fishing as a deck boss on a large trawler. Within five years, he earned his master's license and became an alternate captain on a Bering Sea trawler.

Our middle child, Ahna, at twenty years old, worked a salmon season on land in Bristol Bay. During the summer months, the office in the town of Naknek is the center of the salmon universe. She helped fishermen with housing, meal tickets, fishing licenses, and travel arrangements. I could call her on the radio and get fish reports, and though I couldn't visit her, knowing she was close was somehow comforting.

Our youngest daughter, Kirsten, first came to Alaska the summer she turned seventeen. She worked in the galley by herself on the Columbia, keeping us all fed. Kirdy also grew into being a good tendering deckhand, offloading the smaller gill-net boats' salmon into our large holds. She adapted quickly to sea life and became a favorite of the fishermen delivering their catch. I noticed longer lines at our boat as the Columbia provided the only opportunity to exchange a few words with a cute blonde on deck. A few years later, she worked onshore in Naknek at the "egg house" boxing up salmon eggs, spending sixteen-hour-days on her feet. She met some great kids but seemed happy when the season ended.

After Joanne cooked on the Columbia for twenty-five or more seasons, she joined me aboard a 115-foot Arctic research vessel, the Norseman II, a completely different boat and geographical area for us both. The Arctic was a place I'd always wanted to experience, and I knew the vessel and its owners.

A converted king crabber, the boat housed up to thirty individuals. Two cooks alternated twelve hours on, twelve off. They fed thirty people three meals a day, prepared an additional midnight meal, plus they baked bread, cookies, and made ice cream. The job was hard work, but Joanne loved it.

Together, we enjoyed watching ice floes, walrus, polar bear, and whales. I piloted the Norseman II from Point Barrow, the most northerly town in Alaska, east into Canadian waters. We skirted the Russia/United States border for days, maneuvering through the ice. I took the boat four hundred miles above the Arctic Circle, a thousand miles north of Dutch Harbor, into seldom traveled territory, completely new to us.

Joanne's job was physically demanding, but I dealt with the weight of responsibility for keeping the scientists and crew safe. With endless foggy days and ice floes constantly changing, shifting, stopping, and rotating, I'd monitor ice movement from satellite reports, aerial searches, and a few scant ships' reports. With daylight 24/7, we worked around the clock. I couldn't escape the exhausting mental exertion of monitoring and navigating to reach our destinations without getting stuck in the ice, nor could I relax my vigilance. After the two-month season, I felt like the stuffing had been knocked out of me.

Still, Joanne and I committed to a few more summers on the

Norseman II. Our final season, our youngest daughter, Kirsten, signed on with us. Joanne and Kirdy both cooked amazing, delicious food for the thirty people aboard the research vessel. Kirdy started in the galley at seven in the evening to relieve Joanne and clean up the dinner dishes. When Joanne came on at seven in the morning, she'd clean up the breakfast dishes and begin preparing lunch. Day after day, no darkness, endless work. In 2016, we declined the offer to run the Norseman II for another summer season.

Nowadays, Gus fishes pollock in the Bering Sea, he's married, has two children, and they live a mile from Joanne and me in Bend, Oregon. Both Ahna and Kirdy have since moved on to other careers. Ahna lives in Los Angeles, has a job in marketing, and is married to Zach, a cinematographer. Kirdy is a director for kids' camps in Bend, Oregon and is a gifted video editor, although she is tempted to go back to the sea.

In 2016, instead of the research vessel, I chose to run TV's world famous *Deadliest Catch* vessel, the Cornelia Marie, from Seattle to Alaska for salmon tendering season. Casey and Josh, the regular captains, wanted to take off the summer months, and I looked forward to beautiful bays full of salmon with Joanne in the galley, rather than dodging treacherous ice floes. But running a famous boat for a season is a story in itself. I recently received a call from Sig Hansen to run his boat, the famous captain of the Northwestern, also a vessel on the *Deadliest Catch* TV show.

"I'd love to help, Sig," I said. "But I'm committed to speaking on the Princess Cruise ships."

"Are you kidding me?" He laughed. "Oh man, why would you want to do that?"

I'll always think fondly of those thirty years as a Bering Sea captain. Recently, though, I've chosen a different path, writing and speaking, so others may benefit from my years bouncing around on the ocean, both literally and figuratively.

For now…

EMPOWERING BELIEFS

*What I believe about something determines how I feel, and
my emotions will control me if I let them. To be an effective leader,
I had to change my beliefs to conquer my fears.*

*What beliefs, insecurities, or worries hold you back, scare you, or have
caused you to make a poor decision? If you can be honest with yourself
and consciously redirect your thoughts when that tension flares,
you'll become the kind of leader people want to follow.*

Afraid of What?

"What? You fish the Bering Sea? Aren't you afraid?" asks Jerry, holding his little girl's hand. He's another parent in the school gym, with streamers hanging from the basketball hoops, at our sons' fifth-grade open house. Among the milling adults and kids, Jerry and his wife stand there with their kindergartener, staring at me, waiting for my answer.

I grab a cookie off a plate on the paper-covered table and say, "It's not that bad."

I'd returned three days earlier from two months in Alaskan waters, where I battled thirty-foot waves and was relieved to have survived another season.

The plumber's wife seems satisfied and turns to socialize with another mom she knows, but Jerry squints and tilts his head. "You'd never catch me out there," he says. "You have to hang on for dear life, right?"

I smile and swirl my Styrofoam cup of burnt coffee. "Sometimes, but I feel like I'm designed for it. I love what I do."

He furrows his brows. "No way, man. I watch the TV show. They get hit with giant waves, and the crew gets washed around. Does that happen to you?"

I slowly nod.

Jerry's chin comes up, triumphant. "Ah-ha! I knew it. You didn't want to admit it, right?"

"Yeah, it gets crappy sometimes, but you asked me if I was afraid."

• • •

My mind drifts back to my early years. At age thirty-three, I became captain of a 123-foot fishing boat in the Bering Sea. Though I spent years preparing, the awesome responsibility of making a good catch, while keeping the crew safe and the boat intact, hit me as I accepted the job. Then I nervously placed a call to the Norwegian boat owner who just fired the skipper I'd worked for.

"Do you feel like you're ready?" he asked.

"Yes, I'm ready," I answered without hesitation.

"Vell, okay den. You take da boat out, and ve'll see how you do."

In a couple short sentences, he entrusted his ten-million-dollar boat to me. I had never even docked that vessel.

As the boat's engineer for seven years, I'd watched lots of other captains, many who seemed miserable. They chain smoked, drank endless coffee refills, yelled at the crew, cursed, threw tantrums, were constantly disgusted, always complained about their lousy luck, and drank heavily in town between fishing trips. Captains like this are known in fleet as "screamers." I used to have conversations with deckhands that went like this:

"Hey, how is it to work for Captain Pat?"

"It's money, but he's a real screamer."

"Oh yeah? I've worked for screamers," I'd say. "Better keep your head down and work your tail off. If you survive, it'll pay off."

"Oh, man, he rides us hard. I want the deck speaker to break. He yells at us 24/7."

"Ha-ha, yeah. Try earplugs. Works great to the lower volume. Keeps me from getting wound up."

"Exactly. He stresses us all out, like we're always screwing up."

"Well, just remember, he treats everyone like that," I'd say, and I vowed to be different.

Then my first season as captain showed me a lot about myself. I grew impatient and anxious. I obsessed over other boats' perfor-mances, always comparing their catches with ours. I moved away from good fishing to chase fish I thought the other boats had. I felt uneasy around my crew. Did they like me? Would they leave for a better captain? I lacked the confidence to lead. If something on deck happened I didn't like, I'd yell on the loudspeaker the way I'd sworn to myself I would never do. And I didn't listen. To anyone.

My anger quickly flared if other captains lied on the radio and filled their boats in a location they told me had no fish, leaving me to look for my catch on my own. Headaches became common, and my stomach boiled like a pot of acid. I'd shake the Tums bottle and joke about living on "skippy mints." At the end of each fishing trip, I'd collapse from the exhaustion of stressing day and night, often startled awake, sure the boat was in trouble. I've learned a lot since that first year.

· · ·

Now, standing on the hardwood floor in the school gymnasium feels strange—nothing like the rolling environment I came from and have even learned to enjoy. Jerry's seen every episode about crabbing on TV, which means he's watched the angry, screaming captains, the big waves, the life-and-death drama on his big screen. Thankfully, that's not how I run my boats anymore.

"You don't like to talk about it, do ya?" Jerry's eyes soften and show compassion, like he feels bad for his "Ah-ha!" comment. "It's just, I can't believe you're not scared. Do you get used to hanging on with white knuckles?"

· · ·

That first year, I may have gotten defensive over Jerry's confrontation. In the early days, stepping off the plane, my wife fretted about how my eyes looked sunken and had dark rings around them. Our bank account had grown, but re-entry into normal life had become difficult. I couldn't add two plus two. More than once, I couldn't recall when to pick up the kids from school. I felt emotionally, physically, and mentally spent.

Even as an engineer, I noticed the few captains who were calm laughed a lot, but I seldom cracked a smile. They enjoyed the job and made it look easy. They were also the top producers, without fail, catching fish faster and easier than the rest of us. Being a captain on the Bering Sea sucked a lot out of me, but the good-natured captains seemed full of energy. I had to find out what they knew that I didn't.

At home, I sought books on performance in high stress environments. My search led me to floor traders on Wall Street, where millions of dollars are swapped in a flash via hand signal. Successful traders condition themselves to excel without emotion, often on a subconscious level. I discovered anger, anxiety, stress, and yelling are all manifestations of fear—and my fears controlled me. I also learned my beliefs triggered my fears.

Beliefs are powerful things, and mine sent me on an emotional roller coaster that wore me out. But beliefs are difficult to change. A person will fight for beliefs, even destructive ones, rather than consider something new. Changing my thinking took a lot of effort. Any time I felt anxious or angry, I'd stop and ask myself, "What belief is causing this?" Being honest with myself could be uncomfortable, and occasionally, I resisted acknowledging the truth. Over time, though, I slayed a lot of emotional dragons. The fear subsided because I changed my beliefs.

· · ·

Jerry's serious gaze in his round face waits for me to explain how I cope with the danger.

"I'm not macho," I say. "Our boats are designed for Bering Sea winters. They'll take anything the ocean throws at them. But there are other things that can ruin us."

"Oh yeah?" Jerry chuckles. "What could be worse than forty-foot waves?" His five-year-old daughter tugs on his hand, eager to leave this grown-up conversation.

I smile at her big dark eyes and pouty lips. "Well, you can lose your family. Most guys like me are gone nine or ten months a year. I can be top boat and make a ton of money, only to return to a family who doesn't know me."

"You're nuts, Jack. Who wants to be gone like that, year after year?"

"Da…a…ddy," Jerry's daughter whines, hanging onto his hand with both of hers, swinging her legs around.

"Yep, being disconnected with my family is what I'm most afraid of."

I spot my wife chatting with three girlfriends, a little jealous of how at ease she seems at this event. I feel uncomfortable, even among friends. Re-entry can be a struggle.

After spending the last couple months venturing to remote locations with a small crew, working dreadful hours in a hostile environment, returning to kids' routines, community, a floor that doesn't move—everything seems alien. No one can relate to anything I've been doing either. Acclimating to normal life takes me a week. It's why I call it "re-entry".

· · ·

At least I figured out how to enjoy my job after that first year, which makes re-entry doable now. I forced myself to look at everything in a different light, thinking in probabilities rather than stressing over possibilities. For example, when the weather got risky, I would think in a panic: is it possible we'll sink today? Then I would remind myself that of course, it's possible, but better to ask the more productive question: Do you think we'll probably sink today?

No, probably not.

Besides, the life rafts were in place and the crew was well-practiced in abandon ship drills. I could take sinking off the worry list.

Another question that often plagued me was: is it possible I'll miss all the good fishing? And I would think: it's possible, but it's never happened, so I'll probably find fish today.

That one-word change, thinking in terms of what was *probable,* made all the difference. I stopped worrying about rare occurrences, like a volcanic eruption, earthquake, fire, or man overboard. I let go of emergencies that may never happen by satisfying myself that if we found ourselves in trouble, my crew and I were trained and would be ready to deal with any situation.

· · ·

"Papa." I glance over Jerry's head to see Ahna, our seven-year-old, coming toward me. "Hey, Papa. Mom wants you."

Jerry gazes at me with steady, scrutinizing eyes.

"Yeah, sorry, Jerry. I guess I drifted off for a minute." I lift my cup and glance around for a trashcan. "I gotta dump this cold coffee."

"You're like my dad," Jerry says. "He would never talk about the war, either."

Fishing boats seldom get shot at, but Mother Nature sometimes does her best to show us who's boss. "I'm not fearless. I'm just a regular guy trying to make a living."

"Yeah, okay. Go see your wife, and enjoy your vacation." Jerry looks down at his little girl. "C'mon, kiddo. Let's go find your mom."

"I'm not…"

I start to explain this isn't a vacation, I'm home. Instead, I pick up my daughter and only say, "See you, Jerry," and I walk away with my second-grader's arms around my neck.

**What characteristic is vital for success as a captain
in the Bering Sea?**

I've asked this question on social media and received lots of intelligent answers: courage, tenacity, nerves of steel, cunning, leadership, determination, respect, stubbornness, toughness, competitiveness, commitment, adrenaline junkie, grit, daring, and on and on. These traits are all important, but each one can fail without the key ingredient: **Emotional Control**.

I could possess all the great traits listed above, but if I cannot control my emotions, the roller coaster can overtake those traits in an instant. Thinking of ways to get my head right, and stay cool under pressure, re-created my effectiveness as a leader.

In January 2013, F/V Columbia *offloads a half-million pounds of pollock in the Aleutian Islands, Alaska.*

Photo by: Jack Molan

F/V Columbia *hits a wall.*
Photo by: Kevin Ganley, Capt F/V American Beauty

Research Vessel Norseman II, *115-foot converted crabber. Voyages from California to Arctic ocean up to 400 miles above the Arctic Circle.*

Photo by: Jack Molan

Fishing Vessel Cornelia Marie, *129-foot Crabber. Made famous on*
Deadliest Catch, *the TV show.*

Photo by: Jack Molan

Jack ran Aleutian Ballad *in the summer of 2016. The former* Deadliest Catch *vessel now provides the #1 tour in Alaska, thrilling guests with a close-up experience of the crabber's life. www.alaskacrabtour.com*

Photo by: Jack Molan

Capt Jack and his daughter Kirdy,
250 miles above the Arctic Circle.

Captain Jack lives in Bend, Oregon with his wife, Joanne, but he often travels to give presentations on Princess Cruise ships as well as all kinds of venues on land. He loves to hear from readers, so visit him on Facebook to leave a comment, check out his latest photos, learn interesting facts about wildlife and the sea, and find out about upcoming events.

www.facebook.com/JackMolanPhotography

If you'd like Captain Jack to speak in your community, visit
www.jackmolan.com

76616398R00058

Made in the USA
Columbia, SC
11 September 2017